Mastering Design Thinking

The Systematic Approach To Improve Considerably Your Business Success Rate

MAX ANSWELL

Table of Contents

Introduction

"Design thinking is based on logic, imagination, intuition, and systemic reasoning to explore the possibilities of what could be and create desired results that benefit the end-user (customer).

A mind-set design is not focused on issues but focused on solutions and action-oriented. This requires both creativity and observation. Plan thinking is synonymous with a better future, which aims to build up ideas — as compared to critical thinking, which tears them down.

According to Naiman, development thought advises creativity that focuses on individuals. "Human-centered innovation starts with understanding the unarticulated needs of customers or users," Naiman published in one of his book for the International Business Communicators Association. Naiman pointed out that big business uses design thinking to improve their way of innovating. "Innovation's focus has shifted from engineering-driven to design-driven, from product-centered to customer-centered, and marketing-focused to user-focused," writes Naiman.

For the innovator, the strategic analysis approach helps to reduce the complexity and risk of change by using collective intelligence to improve their awareness of consumer desires through a set of lenses. By also actively engaging with clients or consumers throughout the process using a set of experiments to discover, check and refine ideas, through this dialogue, sharing and through trust, you end up getting closer to consumer awareness to help reveal your needs. Project theorists focus not only on historical data or market research, but on customer experiences obtained from real-world trials and direct engagement.

If you want to make something preferred from the current situation, design thinking helps you achieve this. Through a phase, it gives you. This allows you to reduce risks by collaborating with internal and external entities in search of a new solution that will address a need, problem or obstacle. It happens through a sequence of models to learn from, evaluate and then consistently refine ideas to get them to the finished stage of adding value, eliminating the challenges.

Design thinking lets the innovator achieve insight, identify realistic, achievable, and attractive solutions, design thinking will push user-centered thinking to be integral to the planning of innovators. Project thinking can be viewed in its simplest form as constructing the sequence of transformations that map out the requirements, which eventually becomes the solution.

Continually finding of new concepts for both goods and new uses or resources can be highly supportive of design thinking. It can help answer why a customer buys (or why they change behavior), it can clarify things and make sense, and it can be the catalyst for bringing together insights and concepts. Thus, the concept is a Creative Problem Solving approach that is inspired by the way designers work.

Design thinking can support and become as useful as being part of any (re)design process, institutional knowledge, and technologies. One of its critical roles to play is to make the company aware that it is not the need for internal design; it is vital to customer needs. Customer travel understandings often become component-by-component solutions designed by the specific team participating in that touch-point (customer service, spare or repair portion, billing), but the ultimate execution of any service-oriented system requires a holistic approach, and design thinking can help greatly.

Service design tends to have a higher level of organization and planning. The focus is on understanding increases in infrastructure, communications, and material components. The system development emphasizes the response outcomes with a higher "value, time, and engagement."

What is Design Thinking?

Design thinking is a framework that solves problems and is ideal for dealing with undefined or unknown issues. This makes it very effective in dealing with the multifaceted problems facing the increasingly complex organizations of today. For businesses, in the words of IDEO Founder, Tim Brown, "design thinking is about upgrading within the constraints"–meaning that businesses need to innovate without disruption to drive growth and remain relevant. The successful ones are those who are always looking for new ways in their sector to compete–and design thinking is one framework that can help them achieve this.

We will discuss in depth what design thinking is first in this book. Then we will cover the process of design thinking, whereby we will also go through the five levels of the process: Empathize, Define, Ideate, Prototype, and Test.

What Is Design Thinking?

Stanford Professor David Kelley, who is also the founder of the design agency IDEO, has developed design thinking. The project was also influenced by some professors at Stanford University, Terry Winograd, and Larry Leifer. However, in a study conducted by the Nielsen Norman Group, it is defined roughly the same by most UX and design professionals, regardless of industry and experience. Now, the particulars are not accepted.

A concise phrase defining design thinking would be as follows: design thinking is a human-centered, iterative, problem-solving, solution-based framework.

Design thinking is:

A problem-solving approach: It is a methodology that is ideal for dealing with complex, undefined, or unknown problems. This is because design thinking helps us to define a problem, challenge any hypotheses, and thus framing it in a way that will help us to come up with solutions that might solve it.

Human-centric: We're trying to understand the user in design thinking. This is why, at each stage of the design thinking process, the user–the person is considered.

Iterative: This means that you will use the results to review, question, and upgrade any primary assumptions, understandings, and outcomes at the various stages of the design thinking process. This makes a non-linear approach to design thinking.

Solution-based: The process of design thinking provides a very practical approach to problem-solving. In the scope of the problem being solved, you must devise multiple potential problem-solving methods, model them and check them. Because of the iterative nature of design thinking, until an optimal solution is chosen, you will be able to re-form and optimize these approaches.

Characteristics Of The Design Thinking Process

Design thinking can be seen as out-of-the-box thinking as it allows you to explore alternatives by developing new, and often creative, ideas that you may not have been thinking about. At the same time, it focuses on the needs of the users, thereby helping you address the problem as experienced by the user, including contextual and cultural factors.

Another critical aspect of it is that it encourages inclusive, multidisciplinary collaboration to exploit other people's skills, backgrounds, and thought styles. In all stages of the design thinking process, this will come in handy.

Design thinking, in Stanford's Hasso-Plattner Institute for Engineering, introduces creativity through the integration of three essential components:

- Practical feasibility
- Economic *feasibility*
- Human *interest*

In this regard, and as state, it

- Can help you identify needs that have not yet been addressed–thus presenting new opportunities
- Reduces the risk of launching new ideas as it promotes the idea of failure early and frequently (through prototyping)
- Generates innovative solutions–rather than adding more to existing ones
- It helps organizations to learn more quickly.

The 5 Stages Of The Design Thinking Process

By taking the five-stage approach planned by the Institute of Design at Stanford, you can apply the design thinking method to solve complex problems.

What is interesting about this approach is that it begins with using divergent thinking styles to explore as many possibilities as possible, but then encourages convergent thinking styles to isolate potential streams of solutions. Such five steps, though, are not always linear and can appear in parallel and iteratively repeat. The best way to see them is therefore as phases contributing to an innovative project.

The five stages of the design thinking process are the following:

Stage 1 – Empathize: This stage's goal is to gain an empathic understanding of your users, their needs, and what they care for. To accomplish this, you must put aside any personal assumptions you may have about your users or the problem you are dealing with. You should observe, engage (e.g. through interviews) and empathize with people to understand their experiences, what they value and what motivates them. Also, it is recommended that you get a sense of the physical environment where the problem lies. Such strategies can help empathize with you–an essential aspect of the human-centered philosophy that is learning about development. This stage will inevitably yield a significant amount of information–which you will then have to use for the second stage. In the scope of your project, the goal will be to synthesize all this knowledge.

Stage 2 – Define (the Problem): At this stage, the information you have collected in the first stage should be analyzed, sorted out, and sequenced in such a way that you can better define the problem you are dealing with. In the first stage, if you have conducted interviews, you can analyze the answers and highlight any key phrases related to the issue. This stage will, therefore, make your work clear and focused because you will know what the real problem is. Ideally, if you wrote this down in the form of an issue statement, it would be best. What is interesting is that up to now, the definition of the problem has been shaped solely from the perspective of the users and without any constraints of existing solutions.

Stage 3 – Ideate: You will start generating some rational concepts that seek to solve the problem by using the Stage 2 problem statement. Typically, these ideas are rough–those that result from brainstorming. Nevertheless, they should be valid approaches that might solve the problem being addressed. The important thing here is to "think outside the box" and generate multiple ideas so that in the next stage there are some options for prototyping. You should draw these ideas and present them to users to refine them while selecting certain ideas that are worth further study.

Stage 4 – Prototype: During this point, you will work with your team to create some cheap models to examine and test the potential solutions that have been suggested so far. The aim of the prototype stage is also to communicate something with the team members and other participants, including clients, and act as a framework for interaction. It's important to remember that here, you don't try to find the right solution. You are approaching the issue from several potentially successful solutions. Therefore, considering how to prototype or build a prototype, you should not waste a lot of time. You will pick up and start some supplies. Each solution is prototyped, tested, approved, improved, re-examined or rejected. Not spending too much time and not building complex, expensive prototypes will make it easier for you to let go and move to another. You will have a good idea at the end of this stage of which solutions are most likely to address the problem and what their limitations are.

Stage 5 – ***Test*****:** The successful prototyping approaches were tested using developers, evaluators, and actual customers in the sense of the real product. Testing is conducted to assess each model and to determine the degree to which it solves the problem being discussed. This is a systematic process because sometimes the results of these tests can be used to refine the problem, the prototypes proposed, and the solutions. This leads to further modifications and refinements of the prototypes being tested, moving back to earlier stages. Testing also provides an opportunity for more users to understand and empathize as you observe and engage them. This is also a stage that will help you to refine your way of problem framing and address any remaining preconceptions you may still have. The result of this stage is a sample that solves the hitch and can, therefore, be used as a model for building the real solution.

Design Thinking and the Management Implications

A comprehensive approach to solving business problems is the design process with its elements of open idea generation, multidisciplinary collaboration, prototyping, execution, and continuous refinement. But most businesses don't use it, and worse still, most business schools don't teach it.

Design thinking, combined with group collaboration, is essentially a user-centric approach, project-based workflow, inductive, deductive, and abductive reasoning. The goal of the design process, instead of focusing solely on analytics and rigorous quantitative analysis, is to generate ideas that keep the customer in mind. It involves an almost anthropological insight into how the user perceives, interacts and uses the product or service and how these actions and reactions can best be optimized.

As businesses like Proctor and Gamble, General Electric, Philips Electronics, Apple, Nike, and Levi Strauss become more and more focused on their leaders, adapting a design approach to problem-solving business schools will be entrusted with developing a curriculum that incorporates design.

This shift in thinking and developing curriculum, hybrid models, and strategic partnerships with design schools is embraced by numerous forward-thinking business schools. The Rotman School of Management, Stanford University, Georgetown University's McDonough School of Business and INSEAD in Paris are sterling examples of leading schools. A narrow form of collaboration is currently being taught in business schools. It involves finding and working with someone who shares the same approach and views as you. To foster new approaches and fresh perspectives, the design approach is to work with others whose way of thinking could not be more distinct than your own.

Business schools don't teach consumer comprehension, imagine something that doesn't happen today, model, and continuous improvement. Unfortunately, barriers in business schools to design thinking are prevalent. In many post-secondary institutions, there are abundant semantic gaps, misunderstanding of the brainstorming process, conceptual blocks, and social barriers. Educators also need to take a more interactive approach, rather than the mentality of "I'm right, listen to me," they need to act more as a mediator between student-led groups, offering expert advice and teaching the main outcomes.

The responsibility for adopting a design thinking is not only for business schools but also for businesses themselves, from small businesses to huge multi-nationals. Roger Martin of the Rotman School of Business says, "We are at the cusp of a business design revolution, and as a result, business people today need to better understand the designers, they need to become designers." Company-specific executive education programs can teach problem-driven design thinking, ad-hoc approaches, and leverage in-house design talent.

General Electric Healthcare is sending its top managers to the Ossining, N.Y. Crotonville Learning Center. For the course of technical development. Managers are put beyond their comfort zones, relying on ingenuity, innovation, and strategies to solve problems. Together with the appointment of designers to the executive level, the training program has increased the bottom line and installed a culture that keeps the company at the forefront of innovation.

In many large companies, the success of design thinking is evident. The organization that has seen the greatest success of a design and development thought base is Apple Inc. Despite a weakened economy and the existence of numerous cheaper substitutes, Apple has consistently trumped analyst forecasts and churned out profit quarter after quarter. Jonathan Ives, Apple's VP of Product Design, believes that concentrating on development is a catalyst to create a brand that is simple, elegant, and fulfills a consumer need. Ives has the ear of AppleÊ's enigmatic CEO Steve Jobs, creating products that have revolutionized the personal computing and music industries since the duo hooked up in 1997.

Design thinking can be used in large and small enterprises. The goal is to move away from an established way of thinking and approach a problem or project with the mentality of a designer Ê1/4. As business schools and individual firms begin to recruit, train, hire, and rely on designers and design thinking, with better-designed products and services, the customer will see the direct benefit.

Reasons Design Thinking Should Be At The center Of Every Businesses Strategy Development

How many times did you leave a formal meeting and have doubts that something was going to change? We get together so many times to solve a problem, and nothing is done— it's frustrating. Unfortunately, for various reasons, many approaches to solving business challenges are misaligned— pick your poison. Innovative, business-changing ideas can sometimes be fleeting, but this is the essence of what design thinking helps to address.

Design thinking is a verified and continuous protocol to solve problems that can be employed by any business or profession to achieve great results. Design thinking combines creative and critical thinking that allows organizing information and ideas, making decisions, improving situations, and gaining knowledge. It is a solution-focused mindset, not the problem.

A primary element of design thinking is to think and think about a solution to address a problem or better meet the needs of a customer. It is often surprising and largely overlooked to allow the right amount of time to look through the work being done and assess its value as a viable solution to the problem at hand. I've seen this in other organizations. Surprisingly, it lacks one "small thing," something that's so simple. This reminds me of a large number of salespeople who are not looking for a deal, shockingly.

The insurmountable inertia against positive change can be overwhelming as humans become more assimilated into the processes that govern their company — declines in collaboration; declines in good work born of clear thought. The computer has absorbed every waking minute of the day due to work congestion and unsuitable organizational structures, more often than not. This creates one thing— the chaos of the inefficiency void of new paths. The proverbial "machine" silently does not allow the exact time to move through the thinking process, and this paves a direct path to failure. You're not going to hear it acknowledged by corporate leadership at most businesses, but when it comes to real reform, it's more talk than real practice. Did you know that Google makes it possible for your workers to worry about 20 percent of their time? That says a lot about the importance of learning.

How much do you allow your team to think about good solutions to solve the challenges?

Design thinking should be at the core of the creation of policy and cultural transformation to create a culture that is based on solving problems in this manner. You can apply this way of thinking to products, services, and processes, anything that needs to be improved.

There are many examples of large companies in their day-to-day operations that use design thinking, such as Apple and Google. For all types of organizations, large and small, design thinking can and does work. Yes, implementing in a more established company where processes and systems run amuck can be challenging, but the benefits outweigh the entire bureaucracy cutting process. And for entrepreneurs or small business owners, you need to create and lead a culture of design thinking.

So how do you put design thinking into practice in your company? Let's talk about some of the fundamentals.

Center on the customer; shake well

Don't forget the customer for the sake of goodness. Various functional groups on their own tend to generate ideas that serve the needs of their group more than those of the customer. Their decisions are based on good intentions, but when made in functional isolation, they can sometimes fail horribly for the customer. Fragmented functions are equal to fragmented decisions, and the customer feels their pain long before anybody does it internally. This is so easily fixed, but there are numerous entities that continue to exist. It is important to gain different perspectives, and this is where cross-functional team mixing adds real value, and it is essential to identify those who do it without holding hands. It's one way to help elevate the factor of empathy— a key to isolating and defining the issue. The keyword here is customer-centric. You may be shocked at how unaware of some particular functional groups of the goings-on outside their function.

Here's the good news: Many leaders of these functional groups who are more dialed in may happily shock you, ask a lot of questions, and breach functional barriers without you already. I love getting to know these kinds of organizations. Due to their high esteem, dedication, and awareness of the customer they serve, these individuals excel in identifying solutions. They do right for the customer, live and breathe perfection every day for them, and are obsessed with every intricacy of the customer experience. Unfortunately, management is typically unknown to them. These are the people the company needs to retain the most, but for good reasons, they don't stay long. No surprise here as the performance assessment engine is broken and typically gives the wrong answers.

Identify and define the problem to form solutions around

It defines the right problem to be solved. It is the task of the assembled team to always question the problem at hand and to empathize with the experience of the person they are trying to improve in a multitude of ways. Try to visually represent the problem or scenario around which you need solutions. We are visual creatures, and the better you will be able to "paint the picture," the better you will be able to create viable and valuable solutions.

Create many options for the newly defined problem

Design thinking helps you do things differently— not every time you solve a problem the same way. It is important to come up with many solutions regardless of what the problem is. Be careful that every idea is not overanalyzed. Extract ideas from the brains of all, but be careful not to over-analyze the ideas and thoughts at the onset.

Fine-tune selected directions

Once you have a couple of good options, the group must embrace them. Do not allow things like what happened in the past to discourage you from pursuing a good idea. Design thinking creates an environment that allows new ideas to grow and allows the group to experiment without the risk of mistakes being made. Sometimes it is necessary to combine options, to refine them, etc. It may take multiple rounds to ensure that the correct solutions are given to solve the problem.

Pick the winner and execute

This final stage involves the selection of a course of action and the allocation of resources to achieve goals.

Here are 14 things that you can begin to do now. Keep in mind that this is not a piece of design thinking that is fully instructive. In the past, these are just things that I've seen work.

- Rallying the team in the room–Communicating the purpose, asking for increased awareness of the work being done, requiring everyone to be dialed into the solutions being formed regardless of their functional group.

- Invite everyone to take part in first–everybody should be invited and have the chance to share their voice. Yes, this can lead to a longer meeting, and maybe the focus will sway for a moment, but hearing all perspectives is important because you never know who might have the best idea until you ask. This will also give you a sense of how the group can be divided into different, smaller teams. In the beginning, observe how things happen naturally, and from there, fine-tuning.
- Reduce distractions to zero, no multitasking–for most of us, turning off laptops, cell phones, and computers is long overdue. In your session, ban any multi-tasking as it can easily break the room's thought.
- Recognize when people are checked out–By their function, it is not difficult to detect and most rationalize their behavior. Observing team behavior and finding a way to create the dynamics you need is your job. Speak out of their role to the team and break the damn

format. Require that every person in the room speak and work together. In some cases, ask other people what they think can help, but don't overdo it.

- Accept differences, but don't let them turn into excuses–not everyone is going to be super creative, and not everyone is going to be super strategic. Take these two qualities and merge them to create a magical thing. Accept people for who they are and what is unique about them. Realize, on the other hand, that those who don't speak up might have the best ideas in the room. Living together is all about, and I feel that at the end of the day most people become imaginative and visual thinkers — some need to be encouraged more than others.
- In a good way, lose control. By nature, creative types are breakers of rules. Encourage this attitude and allow freedom of exploration while maintaining problem-focused solutions and metrics for grounding people while allowing creativity for the appropriate leeway.

- No judgment–It is an absolute no-no to judge and criticize thoughts and ideas. It's all gold ideas. Vocalize this rule with your team from the beginning. Help people feel comfortable talking and saying anything. Ideas that focus on a solution and address the pre-defined issue are welcomed. Even the outlandish or stupid ideas can be molded into a brilliant idea or trigger somebody else's offshoot idea. No one should ever be poking fun and establishing this safety net early to increase participation and give you more ideas for detailing and ultimately crystallizing.
- Watch for creeping precision–you may not be able to create a program for space. If you see a trend in ideas far from being solutions to the framed issue, it's okay to throw out a subtle and a reminder to add more accuracy to the idea. You also want to watch for anti-viability trends— don't end up with a majority of valid ideas, but they can't be implemented realistically. Be very careful how this can be corrected as it can be counterproductive and

cause some people not to talk. You can start making final selections after all the ideas have made the board.

- Provide teamwork friction-free and a little enjoyable–Most companies hire project managers to render the moving parts simpler. Sometimes collaboration can be thwarted by having a mediator in the process. We want to chart and report precisely what needs to be done, but at the meeting, we want to make this dimension almost invisible. Design thinking is a process, but don't make it one, please. Watch how the outcome is ruined by a system.
- Give the floor to others–Be careful not to take over the conversation if you're leading the session. In a certain sense, be a facilitator and a mediator. Pass the floor to those who have been working to solve the problem. Engage them for their participation and praise them. Let them come forward with their thoughts and theories and make it a haven. Remember that everyone is creative — give everyone the

chance to speak and come up with a solution or idea.

- Try speed rounds–there may be some goals that can be achieved before the meeting is finished. This is not for any circumstance, but in some situations, it helps. Test the ability of your team to fix something now and bring it to market. Highlight the problem and require a better solution for your team, ready to deliver in a couple of hours to the market. If you're doing a pace game, make sure you mix the best cross-functional group— have all the players on the team that can drive something to market fast absolutely. Try it once, see how it's going, and make a fine-tuning.
- Be better, not perfect–be in good shape with delivering something better than perfect. Also, this is not something that you can extend automatically to everything, but in some situations, you can fix certain things and bring it more to the market.

- Celebrate–Have you been learning something new? Build something the boundaries stretched? These are the things that are going to inspire and should be celebrated — celebrate collaboration on its own. Highlight time savings, cost savings, increased teaming, and anything else that you're proud of with different stakeholders.
- Make it a game–highlight the current score, set the high score you are aiming for, determine how it will be influenced, and beat that score as a team together. Write them down on the wall and pass them over.

Tips on Reaping the Benefits of Design Thinking

You may have heard about "design-based strategy" or recently read about how great success is being seen by design-led companies. But if you're unfamiliar with the term and you're not yourself a creative person, you may not fully appreciate what it means or how it might affect your business. In reality, this business approach can be extremely powerful and can benefit your organization if you have the right talent at your disposal.

For design-based methodologies or principles, there is no strict protocol or set definition. However, it can generally be defined as a way for companies to use creative or design-led ways to solve the challenges of the structure, growth, and innovation. And companies that adopt it properly can better engage customers and adapt to market changes.

As an innovative workplace company, we find that many organizations are highly interested in using a design-focus strategy but lack direction on how to do this properly. That's why when working on a creative executive search with companies, it's best to place a full focus on a detailed and extensive process. To adopt a corporate mindset based on design, the right creative leadership and talent are essential.

The design of any product or service is the basis of any invention or idea that is successful. Due to the mass of brands fighting to satisfy consumers and their growing and changing expectations, the notable emergence of design thinking has emerged. A design-led company strives to enhance the customer experience and focuses on all aspects of its consumer strategy.

Tips on Reaping the Benefits of Design Thinking

Design-focused companies integrate design into every aspect of their brand. Organizations that do this successfully drive innovation and enhance customer experience success.

According to an Adobe study conducted by Forrester Consulting, the advantages of being a design-led company are well worth the investment. 41% of design-led firms attribute more market share to advanced design practices, and 50% of firms report more loyal customers.

Here are some tips from our recent creative executive searches that businesses should consider driving performance and results:

Don't limit design to creativity

Classically, the designers had a very narrow place in the business, a slice of the marketing department's creative team. But designers–and thinking about design–can do so much more. Don't restrict design thinking in a small box or just one specific context under which it can work. It's not a one-step process–every element of your business and strategy should be affected, from user experience to product development to customer service and fulfillment. Design thinking should be taken as a mindset for every aspect of your brand, whether it is developing the product or marketing it.

Design thinking needs to be inbuilt in the organization culture

A design-focused mindset needs to start from the top, with a cohesive vision of the brand and the environment you want to work in. Strong support from the top of the corporate hierarchy is important if the business as a whole wants to follow principles of layout throughout the enterprise. Once this is accomplished, the employees will follow.

A design-forward mindset needs to be present throughout the whole customer journey

Ninety-one percent of technology-led companies find layout an important element of their online customer experience approach, according to Adobe. Just as design-forward thinking has to be ingrained in the whole organization's environment, it has to be able to support any aspect of the customer experience. Do not just incorporate design thinking during the promotional start-up or end-points–it should affect the entire cycle from start to finish (and beyond).

Build a strong team

According to Adobe, to promote innovation, 84 percent of technology-led organizations are investing in tools and services. However, building a team of knowledgeable, creative talent is one of the most effective ways to see desirable results with design-forward thinking. Design-led firms need a reliable team of professionals that are designed-driven to drive business outcomes and innovation successfully. Your human resources are the critical point of departure for any internal plan or system, so a strong talent base is crucial. And keep a steady stream of creativity flowing into your company, don't hesitate and work with a professional imaginative headhunter and recruiter.

Encourage collaboration

Design-led businesses need to encourage and facilitate collaboration within the organization between teams and departments. It will significantly improve performance and results by supporting teamwork and a collaborative work environment where peers can share creative ideas. Facilitate smooth interaction between different teams, and as a corporate initiative accelerates design-thinking.

Focus on your customer first, always

This has become a common position among marketers in recent years, but when companies choose to focus more on their products and services, it is often forgotten. When we're in the innovative hiring cycle, we're also looking for people who recognize the importance of putting customers first, because that's what it's all about at the end of the day.

Talk about it–if there weren't your customers, the product wouldn't. Business and development, the implementation only works when it centers around the consumer. And, when you concentrate on a brand or service's artistic or development aspect, put yourself in their shoes to get a feel of what their needs are and how they can be fulfilled. And don't forget to include them in your design process–this can produce amazing results!

Probes for Context Mapping – How to Design and Use Them

Whether you're making a mobile app, a professional online platform, or an immersive museum show, knowing consumers and how they're going to use your project is important. Traditional methods like interviews and impressions can help you reach their life's surface. A deeper understanding of the experience and desire of your clients comes through generative strategies such as mapping meaning. You need to carefully design the probes kit to use this technique effectively. Read about the three key points that should be taken into consideration when planning context mapping samples to move the designs to the next stage.

People are experts in their own lives and experiences and about them. User understanding is essential to the creation of truly innovative products in their context. We, as developers, can use the context mapping method to inspire and create empathy in the early stages of a project. This technique was defined by Froukje Sleeswijk-Visser, a design researcher and one of the pioneers of the context mapping methodology:

- It allows developers to fulfill the client group's unconscious desires, dreams, and aspirations.
- It contains excerpts that allow users to deliberately present you their environment, their thoughts on it and their visions of its future.

Context mapping examples are tasks we provide in a design project to a target group, from which we can obtain an interpretation of their lives. Probes seek to inspire us as developers at the beginning phases of a project and to sensitize consumers to their context. The way you set up the tasks is important to achieve the rich knowledge you want.

A standard set of specimens contains components for short-term projects. Instead of gathering factual information about them, you must design probes that playfully invite users to share rich clues about their lives.

Stages in the Context Mapping Procedure and how to develop the Best Probes to Fit into it

The context mapping procedure involves **three stages:**

- **Preparing and developing the probes:** I'm going to share the three important steps that will help you get started in the best way possible, and you're going to learn the three forms of probes that usually work well.
- **Collecting:** The main stage is where you collect your users ' feedback, who will have your test kit of tiny experiments and work with it for a few days. Then you will use the outcomes as feedback for the generative session where the goal is to gain a deeper understanding of what your users think,

experience, and imagine through the ideas they make.

- **Communicating:** The evaluation and exchange of feedback within the plan with the design team or other partners ends the process of context mapping and ensures that the design process moves in the right direction.

Stage 1. Preparing – How to Prepare Probes for Context Mapping

Preparing – Step A

Start by setting the cultural probe's goal clearly and selecting the types of probes that match your users. As with any form of development analysis, the most important step is to decide what you need to learn. For example, you may need information in their social lives in addition to their walking habits while developing an interactive experience to get asthma patients to exercise. And when you build an online library system that seduces students to read more relevant literature, you may need observations along with their research habits into their internet activities throughout the day.

The trick is to stay wide enough to inspire design while remaining focused on the problem of design at hand. Many experiments and tests will be more effective than others, based on the objective and target audience. If you want to sample passengers, you can model a package of the specimens that they can easily take with them. Nevertheless, if you want to recognize educators of the 2nd-grade school, you should use a test kit that focuses on classroom drills.

Kquestions to help you get started:

- What is the aim of the cultural probe?
- What do you need to know?
- Which type of probe suit your users?

Preparing – Step B

Build the package so that you hear your users slowly and take them along in your thought path. You need to bring them into it to get people in the right mindset and have them focus on their lives.

The best ways to approach your participants:

Assist them in moving from descriptive to imaginative. In starting to gather some factual information about their behaviors and backgrounds, you educate their minds in making them learn about it in a way they usually don't. They will continue to be more alert to their environment— and they will begin to pay attention to the things you need them to do. For example, by beginning them with tasks like planning their schedule for a given day or taking pictures of their meals, you can later ask them what food targets they want to reach, or what help they need to get a healthier lifestyle.

Assist them to go into the future from the present. Beginning with the memory of actual events and activities (for example, the last time someone made a large purchase) and then identifying and visualizing existing patterns (such as mapping all cash payment incidences), participants are more likely to think about what they want to do differently in the future. As a programmer, you would usually take these steps in your head immediately when someone tells you what a small budget potential payment service would be for users. Your clients have the potential to provide you with these experiences as long as you take them in the right steps for you.

Preparing – Step C

Design to finish the samples: decide how to follow up after collecting the sample kit. Your users have put a great deal of effort into the exercises. You should consider ways to make it more personal rather than having them send you their completed pieces in the mail. Gather the probes kits in person, if possible, to demonstrate your commitment to them. This will keep them engaged and allow them to be enthusiastic about the generational session that you may be hosting later.

Example of a bad Probes Kit

Imagine having a design project that aims to improve the experience of cancer-stricken hospitalized children. Hopefully, the context of a child oncology ward is unfamiliar ground for you, so research is needed. It aims to gain insights into how children view the world, with whom they like to share the experience, and what would make them happier, more involved, and more optimistic.

From a brief interview with the head nurse, you learn they're wasting days in bed, tired and lonely. Building on your children's experience, you decide to design some samples to fit your age group. It begins with a drawing exercise, where they are asked to draw on a timeline, including the people they meet, their daily routine. Instead, they are prompted by a photo assignment to take pictures of their favorite ward pieces. A process of writing helps them to write what they want a day to be like in the hospital. Then, on a pre-printed map, they will draw their dream hospital room — sounds like something a kid might love, right?

Nonetheless, they sleep when you get the kits of the probes from the children. Then their moms and dads tell you they were too ill to do all the things. They've tried to write down your daily routines. What was wrong with that?

You had a clear objective and developed the package to slowly take the kids from concise to inventive and from current to future. You explained all in person and were always at your disposal to answer any questions. They knew that today you'd come around. You did not, however, understand the effect of the disease on every boy. It's time to iterate.

Example of a good Probes Kit

The main things that you realized from the failed attempt were the parents ' constant presence and their role. You will include them in the exercises in the next version of your probes kit. Also, all the tasks are fit to lie in bed, and you take more time to allow the child to sleep for bad days. The revamped package starts with pictures taken in his hospital room by the kid of anything he likes. The parents will give him a reward when he can take at least seven pictures: a cuddly toy included in the package. The child can then draw a circle on a map around his favorite ward places. Then the parents must visit that place and guess what the favorite item is. The parents will get a sticker from the infant they should put into their clothing for every good guess. The kid is also asked to make a postcard to someone in the hospital with whom he wants to spend time, describing what he wants to do. Finally, a story written with the patient as the hero can be read by the parents to their child. Parts of the story allow the child to participate and visualize how the story is going to unfold. Such hints give you all the information you need about the dreams and wishes of these young people.

This time, as you collect the sample kits, you find smiling moms and dads explaining how they enjoyed working with their kids on these assignments. It took longer than expected, but finally, you have the rich insights you need to design something that will make a difference in these troubled lives.

Best Practices: Three Types of Probes that usually Work well

Best practice: many of us choose a one-week time frame because if the process is too long, participants often don't want to engage, but you should adapt it to the needs of your target group. It should take no longer than five to ten minutes per day for each task to complete (or less, as was apparent in the case of childhood cancer). In numerous projects, you may find the below probes useful:

- **Writing and drawing in their context of events or objects.** Write a story about a particular activity of your day or a particular event in the past. You can provide specific text formats, such as postcards or small diaries, to provoke a certain type of text. Provide participants with paper and pencils to draw what is in their heads instead of what can be objectively observed. Drawing is the perfect way to collect your subjective experiences. Give examples of non-intimidating drawing types to make people feel confident.
- **Take a picture of their set condition of the day.** Give the subject, type, and number of photos a focused assignment. If the timing of the picture is essential, give them a trigger via text message. You can, of course, take advantage of it if the target group has smartphones.
- **Mapping their daily routines.** Provide charts with the subject's related indoor or outdoor

areas. Often, to write and draw pens or pencils on the maps. Have some spaces around the maps to make notes if you want to know about their feelings and experiences. The mapping exercise may be part of the assignment of a photograph. You can ask them, for example, to take pictures along their way to work and to show them on a map where they took the pictures.

Stage 2. Collecting – The Main Stage

Now, in the background mapping process, you can go to the next level where you can start collecting your users ' insights.

Collecting – Step A

First, with small practice, you're going to give your users your probes kit, and they're going to live with it for a few days. This step is called sensitizing, as it allows people to become more consciously aware of their meaning and interpret it. They will fill the kit with all the goodness you need for your design process as input. You're going to have a field day looking through them all when you get the kits out. You will set out the packages and try to see trends in front of you. The experts on generative research methods, Elisabeth Sanders, advise to label each piece of information for future reference each time. You can do this by logging the who, where, and when of the information (including the names of the participants).

Collecting – Step B

In the generative session, you will then use the data as feedback. While users are experts in their own lives, they are not designers and are therefore not used to thinking about designs that do not yet exist. The kits will make your users more sensitive, so they are more willing to think about the future and create solutions on their own. You're helping users create thoughts in the generative session.

Collecting – Step C

Finally, you need to engage the users in a discussion. They provided inspirational observations and snippets of their lives with the probes kits. They created new insights on what would fit in their sense in the generative session. By understanding the reasoning behind it, you should complete this information. It will let you to get an understanding by having an open discussion.

Stage 3. Communicating – the Final Stage

Eventually, you need to examine it after gathering all the motivational content for your clients. Sometimes there may appear trends or clusters. Many days, there's going to be a single photo or paragraph. You need to express them irrespective of the kinds of ideas you come up with, or how you find them in the rich data. The observations were provided for fellow design team leaders to move the design process in the right direction. To internalize the need for change, other investors may need perspectives.

According to Pieter Jan Stappers and Elisabeth Sanders, expressing the observations in a way that reflects the target group's dreams and aspirations while preserving their privacy is a challenge at this point.

Design Problem Statements – What They Are and How to Frame Them

What Exactly Is a "Design Problem"?

We've had them all, solved them, and caused them most definitely. But putting it in simple terms is itself a challenge. The Oxford dictionary states that a problem is "a question or condition that is deemed unwanted or detrimental and that needs to be addressed and resolved." Yes, but this means that there is knowledge of the desired result. With due respect for the brilliant minds of the Oxford Dictionary, an important component of this concept is missing: subconscious impulses.

Automobile designer Henry Ford knew about this level of expectation when he said famously, "If I had told people what they wanted, they'd say faster horses." He knew the surprising thing was that horses were too late.

But it wasn't the problem that needed to be solved. His clients were unable to express there was a greater desire.

Richard Buchanan is a "theorist of design" whose career revolves around the principles of human-centered design thinking. In his paper Design Research and New Learning, he alludes to the unarticulated need of a user when he defines design as "the human power to conceive, plan, and produce products or services that serve human beings in the fulfillment of their individual and collective purposes." It is the purpose of the user that needs attention, not just an unwelcome situation. The essence of what a user wants, whether or not they can express it, is this deeper desire.

Ford's clients believed they needed a faster version of what they already had. But Ford understood their purpose more deeply: to move faster from one place to another. This distinction helped him to avoid simply engineering a faster horse, instead opening the doors to create something that had never before existed.

A problem is not necessarily an unwelcome condition or a matter that deviates from the norm— although the meanings of a problem are still valid. An issue is an unmet need for developers and innovative problem solving that, if met, will serve the intent of the client.

Why Problem Frame?

The first step in a human-centered design process is to frame a design problem. It gives priority to the items that have just been discussed: the consumer and the aim they want to achieve. This means that in uncovering deep-rooted desires, an initial round of user research can be revolutionary. Performing user interviews or desktop research, such as competitive analysis, may reveal insights into potential users and what issues they face.

For example, a development question statement may be, "New mums need a way to feel linked to a support group as they spend a lot of time alone with their babies and end up feeling isolated and lonely." These moms have a deep-rooted desire to know that they are not alone, and a new product may help them achieve the goal of feeling connected.

A design team could develop an app, a platform for social networking, or even a brick-and-mortar venue where moms could get together. In navigating decisions and features, the problem statement would guide the team, like, should we use AI? To which other applications should this link? How is it possible to design the environment? The framed question provides a framework for designing the user's best solution.

By framing the problem with a statement narrow enough to focus on creativity yet broad enough, the product design team can remain focused on the problem-solving design and open to innovative possibilities at the same time.

Identifying Barriers and Opportunities

You can see what's in front of you when you know the way you want to go. With a clearly defined issue rooted in the purpose of a user, it is easier to see what barriers are in the way of achieving that goal. And if at the outset of a plan, the issue is clearly stated, it can serve as a prism through which to find additional possibilities that may have gone unnoticed.

Before knowing it, team members — stakeholders, architects, programmers, and even users— have a different picture of what the end product should be in their minds. In a slightly different way, they are both thinking about in different models. How it aligns these varying views is probably the biggest impact of framing a problem.

In a framework that sparks effective conversations and decisions, the process of framing a problem gathers multiple perspectives. Once an explicit statement is made, it is possible to manage group goals and coordinate efforts.

A product team should perform without a given problem— it always happens. But every effort is focused on that single outcome when an explicit statement declares what problem needs to be solved.

A well-framed statement of problem design documented as part of the brief product design is a simple tool for weighing options and measuring success. A good statement of design issues will leave room for creativity, but ultimately it provides a clear lens for viewing each element of the project.

Pointing out the statement of the problem and the steps of the design process act as a filter that sifts out superfluous or irrelevant ideas and retains only those that meet the need. The group will return to the original problem statement as the design process continues to ensure that what is being developed still following the central problem statement identified in the product design brief.

Saving Time and Money in the Long Run

The design process will run more efficiently with a common vision and sign-off on the product's ultimate purpose. Innovative ventures will always have unavoidable tangents and dead ends, but even these examples can be more useful when all is motivated by finding a solution to a single problem.

Operating from a shared understanding of the design issue which needs to be addressed can also avoid public embarrassment— except for a failing product. It was greeted with jabs and jeers as Juicero launched its expensive juicing system because it paid a premium price for what anyone could do with their hands — squeeze fresh juice from a box. It managed to raise

$120 million in funding but, 16 months after launch, it halted sales.

Overall, juice-lovers got very little interest from the brand because it solved a non-existent problem. Not every idea should be executed, and a well-framed statement of the problem can help to determine which ones should remain in the sketchbook.

Helping Connect Emotionally with the User

If you know who is hurting, you can't define an issue. Your team can suddenly step into the user's shoes by taking the time to conduct research and talk to potential users and asking questions about their current situation and how they feel about it.

The emotional commitment required at the framing stage of the problem aligns the product with the person it is intended to serve. The motives, expectations, and concerns of the client will create a framework for all suggestions and initiatives to be evaluated. Seeing a human problem will inevitably illuminate intuitive and emotional insights that make a product more lovable.

Given the significant benefits of framing a question, it is often a missed step. A fully designed design brief, which covers everything from conceptual context to practical specifications, is not unusual to obtain. And sometimes when you join the team, that's all you need.

But if you're at the outset of a plan and the conceptual and practical choices are already being made, it's worth taking a step back to identify the product's question. Sometimes there is plenty of time to do this; sometimes, there is opposition and limited resources. Wherever you are, certain approaches can help give a level of clarity to those concerned.

Design Thinking: Get Started with Prototyping

Prototyping is an integral part of the overall design of Design Thinking and User Experience as it allows us to quickly test our ideas and improve them promptly. The Stanford Institutes of Design promote an "action-oriented mindset" where construction and learning are respected by planning and meeting. But why is prototyping so critical in the phase of design? In fact, how does it encourage you to build approaches to human-centered design? Before we begin to make prototypes to test our assumptions, let's get a closer understanding of what, how and why prototyping should take place.

Imagine this situation: it's an exciting new project, something your team had spent months planning and brainstorming, then perfect building and crafting. You have done everything you could to make sure it was right, with all the features you need. You tried to make sure you put more focus on development and that your text was well made. The website attracted attention and took many potential users in search of the items that you were receiving on the site, but the product and service suppliers were not interested in trying it out. They appeared satisfied to keep doing business as normal, uninterested in the thousands of hits from potential customers that your website received. It didn't make sense to you, but months later you were there, sweating and spending valuable time, money, and resources, and even attracting visitors, but no customers.

It's a story that's told over and over again— ideas are pursued by people with an obsession with making a difference in the market, making big changes in society, or just reinventing the wheel entirely, just to find right at the end of their trip that they've wasted their time or focused on the wrong issue.

This is where prototyping comes in by providing a set of tools and approaches to test and explore ideas properly before too many resources are used. Many of us may recall the art of prototyping from our early childhood, where we created mock-ups of real-world objects with the simplest of materials like paper, card, and clay modeling, or just about anything else that we could get on with. There is little distinction between these types of models and the early rough prototypes that we could create in the early phases of developing concepts.

What is a Prototype?

A prototype is a basic functional version of a proposed solution used to quickly and cheaply evaluate or verify designs, design principles, and other facets of its conceptualization so that necessary refinements or future changes in direction can be made by the designer / s concerned.

This can take different forms, and the only thing that the different forms have in common is that they are all tangible forms of your ideas. These also don't have to be outdated iterations of end products — far from it. Clear drawings or storyboards are examples of models used to demonstrate a possible experiential approach, rugged paper versions for virtual devices, and even role-playing to execute a service offering a concept. Prototypes do not need to be full products: to test the specific part of your solution, and you can model a part of a solution (such as a potential wheelchair grip handle).

Prototypes can be short and rugged — good for early-stage development and training — and can also be fully formed and informative — ideally for near-end testing or pilot testing.

Prototyping involves bringing abstract or philosophical ideas to life and testing their effect on the real world before they are eventually implemented. All too often, without sufficient research or validation, design teams arrive at ideas and accelerate them to final execution before there is any certainty about their viability or possible effect on the target group.

Why We Need to Prototype

Early Research isn't Everything

Research conducted during your Design Thinking project's early stages doesn't tell you everything you need to know to create the optimal solution. Whether you have researched thoroughly and gathered a wide range of information, or whether your sessions of ideas have resulted in what many perceive as a world-changing solution, testing is still crucial to success. Design teams can easily be fixed on the artifacts they collected during the earlier exploration phases, creating a bias towards their ideas. You will expose prejudices and perceptions you have towards your concepts by prototyping and then reviewing those models, and uncover information about your clients that you can use to improve your approaches or create new ones.

Even before other Design Thinking stages, you can use prototyping as a form of research, helping you to identify issue areas for improvement or creativity in architectures, products or services, and spot areas.

Learning by Doing

One of Design Thinking's most important aspects is to test new ideas and to discover hidden perspectives. This is why the curriculum stresses training and events that improve the team's learning ability. By experimenting and exploring the proposed solutions, you can boost action-oriented learning to understand what issues may exist with the hypotheses behind those solutions. As such, your team will be able to iterate quickly, modify your test models, and move you closer to the goal.

Creative Serendipity

Groundbreaking ideas come from nowhere. A Genius spark in a creativity rush? By "sold" to inspire and encourage creativity by way of breakthrough inventions, start-ups, and other revolutionary ideas, one would think that all we need is to flip a switch to a successful mindset.

In their book, Creative Confidence, David and Tom Kelley, founders of the multinational design firm IDEO, discuss the importance of fostering creative serendipity. They encourage approaches that lead to an environment that is epiphany-friendly within oneself. The premise is this: you can open up possibilities for happy accidents by immersing yourself thoroughly within the topic of interest. What this means is that the vast majority of people who "stumble" through breakthroughs do so during their path to connect with the topic area.

The Kelleys quotes different examples of people who made breakthroughs not by thinking through solutions, but by trying things out and figuring them out. Through playing with and testing potential solutions, one of the best ways to learn about the positive and negative aspects of your ideas is to take physical action. When prototyping, you put your ideas onto a physical plane that will encourage you and your team to see and explore the pros and cons, learn from feedback from users, and build little imaginative serendipity opportunities. Stop thinking and get to do it now.

Take Away

Many times we tend to invest in exciting new ideas, brainstorming, and planning for their implementation— until we realize that our brilliant designs have no traction with our users after they have been launched. In other words, the hypotheses on which we based our solutions might have been wrong–

and if they are wrong, they can lead to a significant waste of time and resources. Prototyping helps prevent this from happening. Simple and often prototyping is the perfect way to test your theories, learn from clients, and refine your ideas. Prototypes can be anything from drawings to role-playing on a napkin: anything that allows you to make your designs visible and testable. Prototyping helps create a tendency towards practice (i.e. Creating rather than thinking) and imaginative serendipity opportunities— the innovative catalyst you need to develop genuinely useful and groundbreaking ideas.

Innovative Ideas and Serendipity

With history dotted with depression, recession, and financial crisis, it is easy to assume that because of the lack of resources and funding, innovation is less likely to occur. But that's not exactly the case, because if you look closely at history, in the most difficult times of history, a lot of innovative ideas were conceived. Is that good fortune or luck? It may seem ironic, but these innovations teach us that whatever we have at hand, we can create a working environment that supports good fortune, enabling you to catch "luck" if it happens. This is called serendipity planned.

What is planned serendipity?

Serendipity has been well known in the history of exploration and progress in science, and now there seems to be a resurgence of interest in the transient trend in modern digital life. Is it more prevalent in the digital world? Would Google send us too much, we think we're searching for? Or do we try it out because the sheer pressure of 24hr online society has stifled our ability to recognize it?

In art, chance, or the spontaneous random event, many artists and art movements like Fluxus, Dada, and Situationists have played a vital role in the creative process. Most creative practitioners pursue serendipity and understand the important role it plays in their work and everyday life, though few may have sought to harness the phenomenon, using it as a form of artistic learning.

Serendipity "The faculty to make joyful and unexpected incidental observations"[OED] was first invented in a letter to his brother in 1754 by author Horace Warpole. The phenomenon he named was inspired by a Persian fairy tale,' The Three Princes of Serendip,' who went on a journey of discoveries, connections, and associations, solving problems through their wisdom. "In the elusive role of serendipity and the field of observation, chance favors only the prepared mind," Pasteur describes serendipity with an additional state of receptivity. In the area of imagination, study and training actively encourage receptivity and interest. When prepared, curious and open-minded, it can provide the world with a powerful tool to allow the imagination to leap beyond logic, to develop ideas of intuition and consciousness. This particular research approach, as well as the accidental discovery of knowledge, material potential and positive effect action on it, could be defined as Serendipity and as such used as a painting technique. So what would this mean for the painter, scientist, and adventurer in the art-making process?

Serendipity is a lucky error, a "happy accident" or "good luck." While not specifically looking for it, it discovers something good or useful.

Planned serendipity creates its good fortune by creating a "happy accident" environment. You can face good fortune if you adopt the right framework, not just once or twice, but all the time.

Planned Serendipity: 7 skills

Motion

When Pixar's office was planned by Steve Jobs, he wanted as many interactions with employees as possible. He decided to work with his core services in a central atrium in an open structure. The outcome? Employees struck each other and thereby increased "creative collisions." This type of office makes it possible for employees to inspire each other and generate new ideas.

Preparation

Prepared minds are curious, find meaning in new information, and take things into account in new ways. Patterns are noticed, captured, and open to unexpected connections.

Divergence

Many companies are fully focused on their core markets and services. This kind of vision shuts them off from new opportunities that are serendipitous. Do not close doors; keep your eyes open for possibilities that are fresh and unpredictable.

Activation

You need to activate four shifts to implement serendipity within your company:

- "Ambient shift" means designing your environment to create an atmosphere that fosters new behaviors and thinking.
- Many organizations ' "temporary change" has a more flexible temporality that encourages people to interact in new ways from time to time.
- The "social shift" allows your employees to work together and express themselves.

- The "emotional shift" helps to create an environment that encourages people to be more responsive to the new ideas of each other.

Connection

The more the workers connect, the more chances they will have for productive and creative experiences. It is possible to organize networking events, professional associations, think thanks, sports clubs, charities, and other community groups.

Permeability

Many firms are impermeable fortifications. Organizations should be more permeable instead of creating barriers between workers and the outside environment. Companies are expected to exchange information with employees, departments, suppliers, and customers.

Attraction

The most fortunate people are those who work hard to develop the skills of serendipity. Such capabilities include:

- Demonstration of meaning/purpose
- Development of a clear /reputation/identity
- Development of larger accomplishments

Here are some serendipity examples

The Internet

Of course, as one of the most innovative ideas ever, who would miss the internet? The internet was launched in 1991 when one computer could send a message using the ARPAnet to another computer. Today, the Internet has a significant effect on our lives, facilitating communication through instant messaging and emails. It also expanded our virtual network through social networking, blogging, and forums, and facilitated e-commerce shopping. In the following years, the internet has a lot of potentials to develop, making everything look compact and portable. It only shows that if we explore something, tweak it, dissect it, assemble it again the possibilities are limitless as long as you explore its potential.

The Microwaves

Engineer Percy Spencer worked with magnetron in 1945, electronic devices that create radio signals from the microwave. As he was standing next to a working magnetron, Spencer suddenly felt the chocolate bar softened to a gooey consistency in his pocket. He deduced that his chocolate bar had been melted by the microwaves emanating from the magnetron. This serendipitous insight led to the microwave oven's invention.

Idea Generation

When solving problems and generating solutions, two approaches are commonly cited, namely divergent and convergent thought methods. In a fit of excitement created by post-Sputnik 1, the convergent style of thought was easily balanced with conventional intellect.

On the other hand, imagination was correlated with divergent thinking, and both were viewed as contrasting or opposing mechanisms, not uncommonly. Although divergent thought was seen as good, its equivalent was seen either as bad or a necessary evil that was greatly distorted in industry and education. An important development in recent years is a growing acceptance that real creative production needs divergent thinking and convergent thinking, not just the former.

What Is Divergent Thinking?

The word "divergent thinking" refers to the problem-solving method that is characterized by a multiplicity of possible solutions being suggested in an attempt to identify the one that succeeds. It usually occurs in a spontaneous, free-flowing manner, generating and evaluating multiple creative ideas. A variety of potential solutions are being studied in a short time, and unconventional connections can be drawn. Once the phase of divergent thinking is complete, it is formulated and arranged using convergent thinking, information, and ideas. Brainstorming and creative writing are two methods that contain divergent thinking.

Divergence is typically meant by the ability of a single idea or simple triggers or ideas to produce many or a greater number of complicated or complex ideas. It calls for the making of unexpected combinations, the transformation of information into unanticipated forms, the identification of connections between remote partners, etc. A single question returns multiple answers in divergent thinking, and although the answers vary considerably depending on the individual, all answers are of equal value. Maybe they haven't existed before, so they're new, surprising, or unusual. This is sometimes true purely for the particular setting or the person responsible for the variability in question's experience. In an absolute sense, however, it may also be the case.

Described below are eight elements of divergent thinking:

Complexity – The ability to conceptualize products or ideas that are difficult, multifaceted, many layers or complex;

Curiosity – The characteristic personality of showing sampling behaviors, searching, asking questions, learning to gain more knowledge/information about something, and being able to go deeper into ideas;

Elaboration – The ability to add, construct or embellish a product or idea;

Flexibility – The ability to create varied perceptions or categories from which the same thing or problem arises in a range of different ideas;

Fluency – The opportunity to produce several ideas in order to increase the number of potential solutions or related products;

Imagination – The ability to dream up, invent, or think, see, conceptualize, original new products or ideas;

Originality – The ability to come up with fresh, unusual, unique products or ideas that are extremely different or completely new;

Risk–taking – The willingness to be brave, daring, adventurous–take risks or experiment with new things to stand apart.

Divergent thinking has been detected in individuals with such characteristics of personality–curiosity, nonconformity, persistence, and risk-taking readiness.

Bubble painting, producing artwork, writing a diary, researching subjects, devoting time to reflection and thought, and making discussion lists are all examples of behaviors that cause divergent thinking.

One extreme example of divergent thinking is what follows. Facebook has created an online service that has no obvious practical use. It was then initiated by the social media platform to find out how people used the application so that the application could be refined based on the findings. While it doesn't have to be a bullet-proof strategy to launch something and find out what the market is for it only after the launch (most of the time, it isn't), this seemed to be the case for Twitter.

What Is Convergent Thinking?

Convergent thinking is a problem-solving technique that involves bringing together different ideas from different participants or fields to identify a single best solution to a clearly defined problem. In other words, this is a kind of reasoning that relies on finding the best or often the correct solution to a problem or answering a question. Joy Paul Guilford receives the credit for coining the term "convergent thinking." He came up with the term as an opposite term to "divergent thinking." The focus of this thinking strategy is speed, logic, and accuracy, as well as identifying the known, re-applying techniques and collecting stored data. This approach is best suited for circumstances marked by a readily available solution that needs to be worked out or remembered by techniques of decision-making. A vital facet of convergent thinking is that it culminates in one best answer, which means that ambiguity is not possible. You have either a correct answer or a wrong answer. This form of thinking is also connected with knowledge (one of the key facets of creativity) as it involves using existing knowledge through standard procedures to measure convergent thinking by standard IQ testing. In these tests, reasoning, thinking stream, pattern recognition, problem-solving ability, and skill evaluation can all be tested and assessed. An example of testing convergent thinking is also standardized multiple-choice questions.

Divergent Vs. Convergent Thinking

Below is a study of the two thought patterns of temperament, creative ability, intellectual ability, brain activity, personality, and lack of sleep factors.

Mood – Research shows that preparing for a creative thinking job can result in mood swings that are determined by the type of thinking used for the task. According to the research, convergent and divergent thinking have a converse effect on mood. While the former gave rise to a negative mood, the latter gave rise to the exact opposite–a positive mood.

Creative Ability – In a study with both divergent and convergent projects, imaginative capacity was measured. Although taken as a group, all the tasks showed a connection in the case of the divergent tasks, and they were not important when studying between conditions.

Two forms were used for convergent tasks. The first was duties for remote associates, who presented three words to the subject and addressed the subject to what phrase the three words were related with. The second kind was problems of perspective, which provided certain concrete information to the subjects and asked them a question that called for the shedding of light.

Compared to their counterpart divergent thinkers, the convergent thinkers accurately solved a greater number of the five remote associates issues. A one-way ANOVA found this to be considerably different.

What's more, those who engaged in convergent thinking solved a larger number of insight problems compared to the control group when responding to insight problems. Nonetheless, there was no significant difference between divergent thinking subjects and convergent thinking.

Intellectual ability – To assess the divergent and convergent reasoning ability of teenagers, a series of generic intelligence tests were used. The results of the tests found that subjects classified as substantially divergent thinkers had significantly higher levels of reading and word fluency relative with subjects classified as poor on divergent thinking. Furthermore, it was revealed that the considerably divergent thinkers had higher scores of penetration and anxiety. On the other hand, subjects classified in the somewhat convergent thought classes were discovered to have higher average grades for the previous school year and less of an issue with doing their homework, which means that their parents pushed them into post-secondary education.

Brain activity – In the context of both divergent and convergent thought, changes during brain activity are tested in participants. To do this, researchers analyzed the electroencephalography (EEG) behaviors of participants in the context of divergent and convergent learning. The changes in brain activity, as appeared in the EEG, were different for the two kinds of thinking. Unlike a resting control group, divergent and convergent thinkers created substantial Alpha 1, 2 desynchronizations. While divergent thought created amplitude decreases in the Theta 1 and 2 bands in the cortex's caudal areas, convergent thinking in the Theta 1 band resulted in more right-sided and caudal accuracy boosts. The significant incremental inconsistency and amplitude mean close iteration between the two hemispheres of the brain.

Personality – Correlates in temperament linked to convergent and divergent thoughts have been identified. Results show that two traits of temperament, called Extraversion and Openness, have been seen to make it possible to think differently. Openness analyzes creativity of the mind, interest in literature, originality, liberal attitudes, and imagination. No characteristics of personality are associated with convergent thinking. It means that all people are engaged in a convergent way of thinking regardless of their personalities.

Sleep deprivation – A J.A. review in 1988. Horne revealed that with one night's sleep deprivation, divergent thinking would cause significant deterioration. On the other hand, people engaged in convergent thinking tasks were seen as more flexible terms of short-term sleep loss.

Convergent and divergent analysis are similar in that both reasoning methods are used to solve problems.

Not only that, but the goal of both approaches is to identify the best options. It is often seen that problems are solved by a combination of convergent and divergent reasoning.

Divergent thinking produces the best results when it is used to enable creativity for open-ended problems. Convergent thinking is ideally suited for situations where the best correct answer exists, and it is feasible to determine the answer by evaluating the stored information available. Moreover, although it does not look like the case, it also tends to generate ideas. Since the focus of divergent thinking is ideas rather than process, however, any solution determined by divergent thinking often requires convergent thinking to turn it into a practice to-do-list.

In practice, moving into daily life, this is an example of convergent and divergent thinking.

True, resisting the gravity of the earth to travel in space has been a dream that has existed since women and men first cast their eyes on the stars. However, technology was available only in the mid-20th century to make the dream a reality.

It's an important day in history on October 14, 1957. Sputnik was launched into space by the Russians on this day, thereby initiating the space race. Russia's technology success came to the United States as a bolt. In response, a year later, the country established the National Aeronautics and Space Administration.

In the first half of the 1960s, then-President John F. Kennedy wrote letters to Wernher von Braun and other key people in the aerospace industry. He wanted to know how the U.S. could defeat Russia in the space race. It was only after receiving expert advice on the topic that the president made his famous speech in which he promised to bring a man to the moon by the end of the decade and also to ensure his safe return. The speech helped rouse nearly 400,000 NASA employees and contractors in less than a decade to join hands as a cohesive team to achieve one of the greatest events in history.

Kennedy used data and facts to find out how the U.S. in the conquest of space could defeat the Russians. That was a leading example of convergent thinking. The achievement of this remarkable feat required the development of many new technologies to design and manufacture the rockets, lunar modules, space suits and other necessary equipment. This required a great deal of divergent thinking.

Examples

Here are two more examples that make clear the comparison of divergent thinking and convergent thinking.

Divergent thinking: Mr. A's home is five miles away from the job. He gets 30 MPG from his Chevrolet. However, for both monetary and conservation-related reasons, he wants to spend less fuel on his travel.

Money isn't a problem. What decisions will he make to reduce his intake of fuel?

Convergent thinking: Mr. A's home is five miles away from the job. His Chevrolet will receive 30 MPG. Nonetheless, for both financial and conservation-related reasons, he wants to spend less fuel on his ride. Money isn't a problem. What three vehicles are his car's best replacements?

Both cases can lead to significant outcomes. The trigger for the convergent example might be another problem–perhaps his car was totaled, and he only had a weekend to find a response to the problem. It may take more time to explore the divergent example. However, it may still be possible to find an option that is completely different from what the user has asked–such as designing a vehicle that runs off the air or starting a new business from home.

Differentiation between Divergent Thinking and Convergent Thinking

In our lives, both thinking are vital. None of them is more valuable than the other. They also need to use these opposing mental processes for us to do well in different tasks.

When faced with a problem, different options (divergence) need to be explored. We then limit our options and agree on the "true" (convergence) solution.

For example, John Kennedy used convergent thinking to figure out that by sending a man on the moon, America could beat Russia into space, and NASA's team employed divergent thinking in the development of equipment and lunar modules.

What is Divergent Thinking?

Divergent thinking is about considering several solutions to a particular problem. A term credited to Edward De Bono, a Maltese psychologist, physicist, author, and inventor, is sometimes referred to as "lateral thinking." He suggested that problems should be solved through indirect and creative strategies as one of the leading creativity authorities. For inventive tasks such as freewriting, creative artwork, mind mapping, and brainstorming, this mindset is best used.

Divergent thinking's characteristics include the following:

- Instinctual
- Ideas are generated in a highly spontaneous manner.
- Free-flowing
- Although an answer has been found, the possibility of finding other answers is still considered.
- Complex

- Concepts are multilayered and involve numerous standpoints.

What is Convergent Thinking?

British psychiatrist Joy Paul Guilford coined the term "convergent thought." It refers to finding a certain solution to a problem that has been developed. This is often used in structured evaluations such as multiple-choice items, identification issues, and arithmetic issues.

Convergent thinking's characteristics include the following:

- Fast

Convergent thought is more focused on pace as it seeks to validate the most effective and productive solution in a shorter period relative to divergent thinking.

- Precise

After the method, a correct response is obtained. It means that there may be either a right or a wrong term.

- Logical

A linear method is used and rational steps are taken to figure out the correct solution.

Differences Between Divergent thinking and Convergent Thinking

Direction Divergent thought investigates various external paths, which may lead to a solution, while convergent analysis is quite linear and focuses on the best solution inwardly.

Novelty Divergence focuses on unique ideas or original products of divergent and convergent thinking, while convergence considers the use of previous techniques.

Limit The convergent analysis seeks to find a definitive answer to this question. Divergent reasoning, on the other hand, considers possible responses as infinite.

Certainty Divergent and convergent reasoning Convergent thinking has static sides; black or white is something. Divergent thought, however, approaches ideas less rigidly; it takes into account the gray areas and less definite solutions viewpoints.

Efficiency Divergent and convergent thinking is most effective when it comes to decision-making processes, whereas divergent thought is required to recognize likely options.

Personality Divergent and convergent thinking studies show that people who are open to new and extroverted perspectives often use divergent thinking. It means that convergent reasoning is typically done by both those who are more confident with what is normal and those introverted.

Emotional State Ironically, studies linked divergent thinking with positive emotional states in which depressive moods are associated with convergent thinking. When you become less negative and consider different points of view in a good mood, you are more likely to generate different ideas.

Value of Answers In divergent and convergent thinking, multiple responses are of equal value in divergent thinking. Convergent reasoning, on the contrary, determines that with the highest value, there must be a certain reaction.

Intricacy Divergent thought prefers complex theories in divergent and convergent thinking, while convergent thinking favors strong and clear concepts.

Risk taking Divergent thinkers takes more risks with their adventurous ideas in divergent and convergent thinking as they often like to experiment and go against the flow. On the other hand, by considering tried and tested options, convergent thinkers tend to be on the safer side.

Curiosity In divergent and convergent philosophy, Similar minds seem to be more analytical relative to their convergent peers, as they have several questions and consider large and in-depth concepts.

Brain Activity Since divergent thinking is mostly associated with culture, it activates the right brain hemisphere. As far as convergent reasoning is concerned, it is usually attributed to intuition that is typically formulated in the left hemisphere.

Reasoning Deductive reasoning is practiced in the divergent and convergent analysis as a rational result is obtained by removing other less reliable data. On the other hand, divergent thought tends to inductive reasoning as concepts emerge from a key proposition.

Quantity vs Quality Divergent theory prefers quantity over quality in the sense that its main objective is to generate as many ideas as possible. Convergent philosophy, on the other hand, advocates quality over quantity because it seeks to determine the best solution.

Time Divergent and convergent thinking The process also endures for long periods as divergent thought embraces all potentials. Convergent reasoning, antithetically, assumes sooner because it accepts only what is considered as highly relevant.

Business Design

Have you got an idea you would like to share with the world? An idea is the seed of any business model, and each individual has to share their creative ideas. Any idea is interesting, but it's not all lucrative. In the business world, if it's great and many people can benefit from it, your idea can make you rich.

If you've developed a fantastic idea that can help you earn a lot of money, consider yourself lucky. This gift is not awarded to everyone. The idea of a dropout from high school is sometimes better than the one with a Ph.D. In the management of marketing. Even a remarkable idea can turn into a mistake, though. Once the right strategies are misperformed, an idea is called a fallacy. Incorrect use of a business idea means failure, and every little bit you've spent will crumble before your eyes when there's breakdown.

That really hurts and it's all part of the package it you call life. Any business is a battlefield and the only explanation for any business meltdown is the proper execution of long-term and winning ideas. You need to give the impression that you're around and see what's happening around you.

The goal behind internet marketing is really interesting and the whole process is challenging at the same time. It's still impossible to unravel the mystery behind Yahoo's huge success so far!Reddit, Facebook and Google. Explaining the market scheme used by these companies would take me days. The three main tips are what I can only reveal to you:

1) Inexpensive product

If its products are of good quality, a business is successful. Nokia is still the most popular mobile phone in the Philippines to date, mainly due to its user-open interface, and its rate is within reach of many.

2) Advance services

There are several good services for Internet users out there on the following websites listed above. Not only is Google a giant search engine, but it also has other apps such as Gmail, AdWords, AdSense, Analytics, Docs, Planet, Maps, Speak, Translate, etc. Feel free to explore several services offered by Google. They're free and user-friendly.

3) Distinctive

A market is considered special if the goods can still outshine other rivals among the companies. There are a variety of search engines on the Internet today, and I have a question for you: can you conceive of why Google is so different from them? Is one of the reasons for its distinctive name?

Although, in a general business degree many students will be major, anyone who has taken business courses will realize this is an extraordinarily broad term. You will be required to choose from a variety of specific business designations at some point throughout your studies, in most cases. If you are still unsure about which area you want to go through or are considering a career change, you will want to weigh all the choices carefully before looking at additional training programs to know more. General classification examples include finance, marketing, public relations, business development, or administration of transactions.

The benefit of a general business degree is that it offers you an overview of a large number of these specific business designations, which may cause you to choose one specialization that you love more than the others. Of example, if you love math and accounting, you may want to be licensed as a public accountant or as a procurement director. However, some other people may rather enjoy the sales side of the business side. Marketing or creation could be better bets in those situations.

Even if you are not attending a full university program, by attending various certificate programs you can still learn more about your choice's business designations. Those who are already in the workforce will profit most from this because they can be done from the comfort of your own home in your spare time, and then lead you in the office in a completely new direction if you want to change your profession. Even if you just want to find out more about your new choice field, this is a good way to explore your options before you make that move.

To find out more about these different business designations, the first step is to find an online program that works best for your needs. You might consider combining or taking the designations one at a time, although some course may overlap with the curriculum. If you're unsure, that's something to ask about in advance. Also be sure to ask about the credentials of the instructor for each program, find one that is adequately qualified to teach their specialty of choice, and how long it takes to complete the program. Some will only be a few weeks, although more comprehensive information tends to be available in programs that last a few months.

Businesses are sure to have an outstanding impact on a professionally designed logo. Big organizations pay extra attention to brand distinguishing or logo design, as it is something that helps them to be noticed and beat the competition. The simple rule is that the lower your logo's class, the lower your company's figure. It's a good thing that you want to appreciate your business, although by creating a high-class design, you can either have your business well-known or make it unreputable by having a low-class design. So when you're all ready to build your brand image, you have to be careful.

A research must always be the initial step. You must check the designs of your rivals ' brand identity and evaluate their professionalism. Are they outstanding in class? Can they get a good idea? Do they seem to be an expert? The reason for this research is simply to gather statistics and verify your competitors ' tactics. Do not make the mistake of replicating your competitors ' models, as you will inevitably get trapped and make a really appalling impression. The work must be conducted for the sole purpose of thought and imagining. You have to stay miles away from copying to make sure you're producing a unique design.

You need to come up with a plan to design your own logo after you examine the designs. The critical goal of having a much better logo design will beat the rivals. Individuality is something you should not give up. You should do some brainstorming and consider how to make a design that is completely unique. If you don't have any design activity, it's better to engage the brainstorming process with your client. Through special designs, the developer will be able to offer you and make you stand out from the rest.

Talking about a logo designer, make sure you only get an experienced designer's knowledge. Your logo is not something that you will change every few months afterwards. It will continue for years to come with you. To do the job properly and pleasantly, you must employ an expert designer. A neophyte designer will give an immature look to your business and you will end up losing your market confidence. If you want to convince the audience that you are a real professional, so you have to make a professional logo and only a professional logo maker can make it.

Logo design is a key component of any advertising campaign. Marketing campaigns can't be successful without a logo design, because the audience won't be able to identify you without your logo. Whether you endorse your business online or offline, it will be with you all along your logo. Not only will it give an image to your company, it will also help your business in an efficient way for you.

Conclusion

Business Design offers business people and executives with a viewpoint to think creatively about and better grow their business model. The systematic approach makes it possible with few resources to test the viability of new ideas. This will be the critical competence in the future that will decide on an accelerating market's success.

Developing Skills for Life through Design Thinking

Inquiry questions, open questions, creative questions, questions that are closed, questions that lead. A couple of weeks ago, we questioned "questioning" at our family dinner table. Sabrina, our daughter of 8th grade, told us she worked at school on inquiry questions. As a typical teenager, she asked whether spending hours doing this is useful. We were curious to know exactly what these questions were and how you formulate a successful one, to offer a "correct parental response." Our questions led to an "art of questioning" discussion. I thought later that night how lucky Sabrina is that she is already learning about and–even better yet–using Middle School questioning skills in different classes.

We had just had this talk when Christen Wilson, Head of Advancement, Advertising & Communications at

The Magellan International School, asked me if I would write a school blog post about "the skills that our school develops, particularly those that will be incorporated into development thinking processes and training for continuing education, life and career."

Our kids will face a world that is changing faster than the world in which we started our adult life. Our world is already full of big challenges, and our kids are likely to face even bigger challenges. Introducing Design Thinking, an effective method of solving complex challenges, at a young age, is a benefit for children. They will learn how to be innovative and build trust in their ability to solve creative problems. Experienced design thinkers also have an open mind, a growing mindset, empathy, and well-developed thinking skills. I hope that these talents and their imaginative ability will make our children more resilient and allow them to succeed as adults in their professions as well as in their personal lives. Yet Design Thinking is not unimportantly enjoyable and can increase curiosity and interaction with school and learning.

Why Are Innovation & Creative Abilities So Important?

Over the past few years, innovation has been a hot topic in the business world and will continue to be top of the business list. With the pace of technological developments, the exponential amount of information and resources at our fingertips, the integration of increasingly artificial intelligence into our daily lives and globalization, companies are constantly being forced to innovate to remain competitive in their markets.

The number of global challenges we face in preserving our planet and natural resources and providing our ever-increasing world population with opportunities to live safely, be healthy, and have meaningful lives is just as pressing for us to be innovative.

Knowledge and information are already available everywhere and on an ongoing basis. Access to information and knowledge is no longer the one-time strategic strength. To be able to effectively use information, knowledge, and artificial intelligence to solve problems, innovate and improve lives, workplaces, and ultimately create a better world is becoming more and more valuable for companies and individuals.

Skill Building Through Design Thinking: Creativity, A Growth Mindset and More

Through my work at THINK Creative Leadership school as an Endeavor Coach, I have had personal experience seeing how leadership in innovation can have a positive impact on your life. I noticed it in myself and saw it in the school's participants. THNK has developed an approach to innovation based on design. Through a real-life global innovation challenge Design Thinking can help everyone to be more creative and innovative, adults at THNK are encouraged to become better creative leaders by working both on their personal creative leadership development and learning techniques, approaches and methods. We can all create something useful through its practice, and it stimulates the development of a mindset of growth. The concept of a growth mindset has been developed by psychologist Carol Dweck.

According to Dweck, "In a mindset of growth, people believe that they can develop their most basic skills through dedication and hard work— the brains and talent are just the starting point. This perspective promotes a love of learning and strength that is necessary for great accomplishment. "By being introduced at such an early age to Design Thinking, our children can feel the ingenuity that is in us all playfully. It's not just something artists do; we can all be creative. So our kids will see that imagination is useful not only in making art but also in solving everyday problems. Design Thinking helps us find our creativity and use it.

Creativity is also a skill established from experience. You can't just read or learn about it by watching videos from YouTube. So it's wonderful that we now have a school maker lab where the kids can prototype or build some of their solutions.

You can develop a lot of other skills through Design Thinking. Learning others, asking, learning that is divergent and convergent, collaborating in groups–to name a few. Technology designers cultivate useful features such as being open-minded and empathic, and they tend not to be afraid of failing, but rather to see failure as an incentive for learning.

Understanding People, Developing Empathy

Design Thinking is a human-centered approach, which means it starts with individuals and ideas are adapted to their needs. It requires you to really understand your users and to design a solution that is personal and specific. It is necessary to adapt and understand the users ' habits, preferences, beliefs, activities, etc. You examine how they work, what choices they make, how they live and work, and find out what they really want or need. The kids can gain greater empathy and compassion by learning to take the user's view.

The Art of Questioning

Sabrina explained to us at the dinner that inquiry questions are used to shape the content of what will be learned this trimester by her class. In science, she has used these kinds of questions a lot to set up her research projects–they need to be open enough to require research, and that often involves a comparison of things to be effective.

To the creative questions used at THNK, we compared the inquiry questions. A creative question is used in a challenge at THNK at the beginning of the innovation process. A creative question will help guide the team's work. It is broad enough to stimulate an in-depth examination of the topic or problem area to allow multiple directions for a solution, but narrow enough to address the specific problem.

Asking questions require you to immerse yourself in your topic, and it helps you find your connection and fascination with the topic. What makes you more eager and determined to develop a good solution is to have a personal connection. It means "to find out why you care about it."

In The Inevitable, Kevin Kelly sees questioning as "one of the larger forces that will revolutionize the way we work, play, learn, buy, and communicate with each other." He writes that almost all questions can be answered cheaply in the future with all data, information, and knowledge on smart machines. A good question is asked about the challenge and the task that computers are likely to be able to perform last. The right answer is not a good question, but one that questions current responses creates new areas of thought, and that can be a test, a what-if scenario. He states that in the future: "Question Makers will be better regarded as the drivers creating new areas, new industries, new brands, new possibilities, new continents that our ambitious race will discover."

Being Open-minded

Questioning the status quo is an important start to the process of design thinking. It guides the way you look at an issue. Years ago, as I started my career as a consultant, by starting with a hypothesis, formulating possible solutions and assumptions, we approached every problem. During the project, we'd explore how to challenge the assumptions and our solutions or find facts to support them.

The Design Thinking process, on the other hand, begins more openly and with a wide-ranging survey of the topic before you begin, formulate, test, and prototype your solutions. Given the current world problems are very complex, often interconnected, with diverse stakeholders and often on a global scale, a more human-centered, integral, broad approach to problem-solving is becoming increasingly important.

To examine a situation broadly requires us to be open-minded: ready to hear the ideas of others, and challenge our hypotheses, able to examine our own biases, and curious to try new things.

Working in Teams – Being a Team Player

The Design Thinking process works best in teams, as multiple viewpoints are required for the process. New and better ideas and solutions will be produced by a diverse team. Thinkers of design know this. They have learned that the creative process is made possible by various teams. And diversity needs to be represented in many ways: background, knowledge, expertise, interests, preferred (structured and unstructured) way of working, way of thinking (convergent and divergent), types of personality, etc. Working in a team encourages us to be good communicators and help each other achieve success.

Working in teams allows us to learn how to deal with tension and how disagreements can lead to even better solutions. It also introduces our students to circumstances in which teams succeed and, most critically, to situations in which a team suffers or struggles. It's invaluable to learn what you can do to make teamwork better at school, at work, and home.

Failing is an Opportunity to Learn

The team designs test and produce a prototype of the solution in the prototyping and testing phase of the process. The prototype is tested with the users themselves. The team learns what works well and what doesn't work through prototyping and testing. It's as important, what doesn't work as what does. It's not bad if the prototype fails because it offers the chance to learn what needs to be changed or improved. Design Thinking requires different process cycles leading to a final solution that will solve the problem of the user and give them what they need. This is a proven process in business today; you don't over-engineer solutions, but start with a good prototype and improve it with input from real users in the design process.

The processes of prototyping and testing teach us that failure is okay. Small failure is better and learns from it, then big failure. Even worse are cases where the team is not doing anything because they are scared of failing high.

Naturally, children are risk-takers, they try to fail, they get up, and they try again. Design Thinking should allow them to keep up with this tendency and use it through life and career to their benefit.

Business Innovation - Turning Problems Into Solutions

Problems, problems, problems-if we never had any problems, life wouldn't be great. Everything would work perfectly, everybody would always get along and be happy, everywhere, everything would be wonderful for everybody, and things would only get better as we live happily.

Unfortunately, the grim realities of the dark side are not avoided in the real world. From a business perspective–take every person's number of problems, subtract by the number of employees, multiply the outcome by every part of doing business, and the result is what has the business owner biting their fingernails to the bone.

Eliminate the source is the most commonly accepted way of solving problems. But this method is not always as straightforward as it seems. It can be a very difficult job to determine the true cause of a problem, and even if you get this right-removing the trigger will create a whole new set of problems just as quickly.

Wouldn't it be good if a company was free to implement policies and procedures that would solve problems on its own, and the business would benefit tremendously in the process?

How Problems Can Solve Themselves

It's all about turning disadvantages into benefits accomplished by finding innovative ways to look at issues from a new perspective. A slight change in perspective is all it takes to show as seen from a different frame of reference a whole new range of possibilities.

The Value of Business Innovation

For a while now, creativity has been a buzz word bandied about the business community. In fact, over the years, the concept of innovation has flourished to become itself a whole industry.

What is creativity in business? In terms of creating new marketable innovations, the more traditional view will describe corporate creativity. Business technology is also commonly associated with the research and development practices involved in the design and promotion of new products and services.

As the marketplace becomes increasingly saturated, innovation plays a vital role in distinguishing your products from the competition and taking advantage of every available resource to gain a crucial competitive advantage. The modern view acknowledges the strategic value of implementing technological technology in EVERY step of a company's infrastructure which encompasses the entire market context.

Establishing a Culture of Business Innovation in the Workplace

Within a pyramid structure, market creativity cannot succeed if it starts at the top and spreads through an enterprise with declining frequency, hitting close to zero at the bottom. A more effective strategy would be to invert the flow so that business innovation begins at the base and accelerates continuously as it gains momentum on the way to the top.

Establishing an innovation corporate culture throughout the workplace begins by promoting a proper management attitude. Innovation is about understanding interest in the versatility factor and accepting the task of responding in a constant state of change to circumstances.

Abolishing the Status Quo

For those who are used to the mental comfort and security of merely maintaining the status quo, this form of freewheeling behavior can be challenging. Innovation is generally applied incrementally in small "safe" steps of the baby, and only to streamline established procedures rather than to risk the potential impact of major change. Major changes usually occur only when the old tested techniques become inadequate and redundant.

The Hallmark of Creative Genius

Everyone has the potential to develop the type of refined mental flexibility, which is the hallmark of creative genius, given proper training. Sadly, the traditional formal education program does not include this level of specialized training. Training cultivates a very linear thinking style. As a consequence, we are all born with innate childlike resilience due to abuse. Adults endowed with creative genius are those who, despite the destructive aspects of education, have nurtured their mental flexibility through their own volition.

Companies would be well advised to look for these rare individuals for key management positions, not just for their own creative input, but more importantly for their ability to recognize the value of innovative ideas that others have contributed. These are the best-equipped people to lead the effort to develop effective strategies to successfully deploy new ideas.

Despite the suppression of our creativity, it is not completely lost. The realization that everybody has their eureka moments of inspiration from time to time thrives on a corporate culture that endorses perpetual innovation.

Removing the Impediments to Innovation

Frontline workers see a company from their unique perspective, and rightly so, because every day's working hour, they are intimately involved. They often see management problems not and see how the company could benefit from certain changes. In fear of causing negative repercussions, many are reluctant to come forward. Frontline staff is prone to the threats, not to mention their entire career, raising the wrath of those with control over their position in the company.

Those in management positions often have the impression that they are the ones who do the "reading" and that frontline worker are paid to work-not to dream, have opinions to question validity of existing policies or procedures. This form of criticism is often seen by administrators as a challenge to their integrity and power that could undermine their status. Corporate cultures with a rigid hierarchy create a working environment in which all develop their private self-serving agenda that is often out of sync with the best interests of the company. A hierarchical hierarchy threatens to stifle innovation, causing the other side to lose significant incentives.

A critical factor in cultivating a culture of business innovation is to remove intimidating factors of fear that are endemic to the more common authoritarian culture so that employees can truly feel free to contribute ideas. Indeed, new ideas should be encouraged to contribute, and employees should be rewarded for ideas that are adopted and prove beneficial to the company.

A business will actively recognize tremendous benefits by encouraging everyone in the organization to dedicate a small percentage of their workweek solely to creative production. Performance resources and preparation should be offered to optimize their potential for success.

It Starts at the Top

Even the most innovative company technologies are worthless without the commitment of the central leadership to implement improvement. It is the high-caliber management vision and power that defines the overarching ideology of an organization. There comes a time when a company needs to challenge this philosophy itself to evolve with a changing marketplace.

Success in deploying an innovation culture depends entirely on cultivating EVERYONE's proper attitude within the organization, and no exceptions can be made. It's our rigid preconceived notions of how we think things ought to be that keeps innovation from working its magic.

Plant the Seeds and Reap a Bountiful Harvest

One of life's precious few unchanging facts is that all changes. They succeed in recognizing that each hardship has the kernel of a new opportunity. The current economic crisis is just another example of a transition that threatens our ability to innovate, adjust, and take advantage of the new possibilities that change provides. As stated earlier-it's all about transforming the drawback to advantage, and all it takes is a change in perspective to a different point of view.

We need to be willing to continually re-examine and re-evaluate the truth of our existing perceptions to determine how to shift our perception. Innovation is the means of moving past our existing expectations to explore new opportunities-rich areas. An organizational creativity culture is the means to make good use of any organization's most important asset-its employees. There is nothing stronger than open hearts and open minds working together for a common purpose in synergistic unity.

Any company that plants the seeds of change throughout the entire organization will certainly prosper and reap a bountiful harvest, supplying all the resources needed to sustain new growth, and removing any hurdles that obstruct new growth.

Conclusion

Innovation and creativity both play a major role in a company's success. Business processes can be enhanced by using innovative ideas, productivity can be increased, new products can be created, and competitiveness can skyrocket. Companies need to constantly foster an innovative environment, even if it means investing in it in difficult economic times. By doing so, they will be assured when the economy improves that they will be in a competitive position. The business world is highly competitive, increasing the value of innovative ideas than ever before.

Advantages of an Innovative Environment

Innovative ideas can be helpful in a wide range of ways for a business. Productivity can be increased in some situations, which can allow a corporation to lower costs and become more profitable. By creativity, alliances, and collaborations with other firms, clients, vendors and even sometimes indirect rivals can often be strengthened. Organizations also often find new ways of marketing and developing their products more efficient. In some cases, the implementation of an entirely new product or service could be an innovative idea. In many other situations, though, it could simply mean a series of small improvements that strengthen a company's way of doing business over time. This way, companies pursuing and promoting creativity in industry are in a much stronger position to compete and thrive.

Lack of Business Innovation

Just as there are distinct advantages to undertakings that foster a creative environment, there are also distinct risks for undertakings that do not. In many situations, a lack of innovation can lead an organization to lose market shares of its rivals. Efficiency and productivity are going to fail, mostly resulting in lower profit margins. These businesses are also at risk of loss of employees, spanning from core workforce key staff members. Businesses were even known to leave the business in a worst-case scenario due to a lack of innovation and creativity.

Balancing Business Tension

So, you're ready to start your company, but you're not prepared to give up your day job. Perhaps you plan to use your income from your day-to-day job to help fund your new business or rely on that income to sustain your living expenses until your business can generate a profit.

Whatever the reason, this is precisely how many entrepreneurs have started their business. Although it's a tried and true way to get your business going, it takes a lot of hard work, long hours, and maybe a couple of complaints along the way. However, it is not only possible to start your business at the same time as keeping your day job, but it is also often a smart decision.

Tips for starting a business while keeping your day job

If you have issues with your material and you urgently need an expert report on content analysis, how do you decide what service to use?

Choosing a company or consultancy to evaluate content can be a daunting prospect, mainly if you have not previously engaged in one. While many companies may claim to be masters, before choosing one, there are several different aspects to consider.

Ideally, following our advice would encourage you to choose the right organization to solve your content issues and make sure that a practical and easy-to-understand content analysis document is beneficial to your business.

Recommendations

The best type of reviews that can be obtained is from trusted friends, superiors, or other employees, but these may also be the easiest to locate. Depending on the circles of people you associate with, the chances of knowing someone who has even gone through a similar content analysis as you need are potentially quite slim.

The second best choice is to contact a former client directly, or read their comments and testimonials. There are many ways to do this, and you should be able to find any user reviews relatively quickly when searching online.

When you can't find any comments about the service, the alarm bells in your head should be set off. While this particular company may be new and therefore has no online reviews, until working with them, you should do more work.

Experience

Experience is crucial when it comes to the analysis of content. It is a sage and advised decision to ensure that the agency you chose has not only strong general research expertise but also information in your particular sector.

Successful content analysis is carried out by a company that usually has a vast background in the industry. There are many different methods and areas of expertise, some focusing on one type of content, such as web content, while others, such as technical writing, will be specialized in a different area.

Consultation

As a guideline, without any initial consultation, you should not pay upfront for content analysis as you should make use of the companies offering a free one.

A good, professional and leading firm will want to show you what they can give, so be vigilant about any corporation that doesn't want to work on your behalf without first receiving payment.

Value for money

The last aspect to consider when looking for a business to carry out an evaluation is to weigh the cost against the work quality. It is a smart idea not only to choose the cheapest option, as it is far more essential to ensure that the project is done accurately and comprehensively than to pay less and end up with poor content analysis.

Commit time in advance for work on your new business

As you focus on your new business while still managing your full-time job, time can often be shorter. Therefore, getting a routine is crucial— and just as necessary, actually going through it.

"Build a plan before the days and times you devote to working on your new venture and, most critically, stick to it," says Aqua Mobile Swim School's Diana Goodwin. "Otherwise, it's too easy to relax or let yourself be overwhelmed by other tasks at the end of a long day." By splitting your time into manageable chunks, and devoting a certain amount of time each day to your new business, you can make it easier to combine the two. "The hard work will pay off if you can work on your own business full time, do what you love and be passionate about it!"Say's, Diana.

Cut back your hours at your day job gradually

When the budget and your work schedule permits, consider reducing the amount of time you spend in the workplace and using those afternoons (or even full days) to focus on your new venture exclusively.

"If at your day job, you can start cutting back on hours, just two or four days a month, then begin the transition process now," says She's Got Systems ', Kelly Azevedo. "With one day a week to focus entirely on your job, you're going to be much more successful and willing to adapt to the change in income." While this won't be possible for everyone, if your workplace provides any flexibility, this could be a great compromise; you won't have to choose between feeling completely overworked and giving up your full-time show. "We usually see day-to-day work as all-or-nothing," says Kelly, "but with this approach, during the transformation you can get the best of both worlds."

Don't get discouraged, but do know you'll have to make sacrifices

There's no way around it— it's hard to start a business. Starting a business while working elsewhere? Even harder. But once you realize and accept this, it will be easier to recognize that the hard part is par for the course at the beginning.

So, don't let it discourage you because you can't give your whole time to your new business. "Most people think they cannot start a business until they invest 100% of their time on it," says Jonathan Long of Market Domination Media. "Of course, it's going to take a lot of energy, and you're going to be mentally and physically exhausted, but as long as you fully understand it early forward, you will make it work." He also says that while you don't have to worry because you can't give your new company all your time and effort, certain stuff will eventually have to be put on the back burner for a while. "Get ready to give up your social life as well — your new venture will take you all your time away from your day job," says Jonathan.

Make use of your daily job to pay off debt and generate an emergency fund

If, while starting your business, you are still working at your day job, use that security to your advantage. "I know so many people who have started a business while keeping their day jobs," says Allie Siarto Photography's Allie Siarto. "They often felt ready to make the jump into running their businesses full time after they had paid off their debt, and had enough money in the bank to give them a six-to twelve-month runway of living expenses." Having a steady income from your day job allows you to make the best decisions for your new business— something you might not have if you dropped it all and devoted your whole time to it. "Benefit from regular paycheck, and save as much as you can, so you don't make fear-based decisions," says Allie.

Meet with a lawyer to make sure you're in the clear

There are some practical issues that should be taken into account when you launch your business at the same time as holding your day job. Many businesses are going to be extra careful about your actions (even what's going on outside the office), so make sure the new venture won't cause you problems.

"Something as apparently innocent as sending a private Gmail email to your company laptop could spell trouble down the line," says ZinePak's Brittany Hodak. "Even if you're starting a business that doesn't have anything to do with your day job, it's worth consulting with a lawyer to make sure you're not setting up for any problems," Brittany recommends sharing your current employment agreement with your solicitor and the plans you've got for your new startup to make sure you're not setting up for conflict.

Set a monetary goal for when you will quit your day job

Set a financial target and use it as a catalyst to put a bit of gentle pressure on yourself when you're going to focus on your new business. This can either be a saved amount from your day job or an earned amount from your new business— or both.

"Have a clear financial target set out so you can leave your day job as soon as you hit it," advises Start Ranking Now's Nicole Munoz. "Use positive language for yourself, such as' I'm going to leave this job when I'm earning $10,000/month' to help you achieve your vision." Dave Nevogt of Hubstaff also recommends setting a target based on your daily work earnings. "Use your career as a temporary safety net and save what you know you'll need to live comfortably for at least 12 months," he says.

David also points out that saving for your new business may not be as hard as you might imagine, with such a complete schedule. "You're going to dedicate your free time to grow your business and go out less," he says.

Note, this step is not going to last forever — the financial target will serve as a jump-off point. "Once you've built up your runway, leave your job," David says. "It is important that your company should also make you profit by that level."

Manage your free time well and minimize distractions

While not working yourself to death is crucial, running a business while still working at your daily job will mean crunching a little bit of time for a while. As such, concentrate on better time management; once you remove the pressures, how many things you would pack into your day would be surprised.

Money Crashers Personal Finance's Andrew Schrage has the following suggestions: "Use tools like LeechBlock to block access to websites that annoy you (including social media), use your lunch hour for short errands or a fitness workout, and cut back on tv and social media," he states.

Budget for fatigue

If, throughout this article we seemed a little "doom and gloom," it's because the reality of the situation is that it's difficult to start a business while maintaining your day job. "To have a day job and start a business at the same time is not an ideal situation," says

SupportNinja's Cody McLain. "You're going to bad risk-taking decisions and hurting your reputation because both commitments are bound to bleed into each other's time." However, focusing on the bigger picture is important; the time you spend starting your business now is going to pay off in the long run. "Remember, when your small business grows, you'll have plenty of free time, and you've left your day job," says Andrew.

It's an important reminder; the late nights, the stress, and the packed schedule you're experiencing at the moment are all leading to your dream of running your own business.

Top Attributes Elevate Design Thinking Leaders

As a business advisor, I strongly believe that the key to long-term viability and success is continuous innovation and design thinking. Recent surveys of global business leaders indicate that they are largely in agreement, but less than a third feel that the structure and management of their companies are ready today, they and I are constantly looking for ways to train present and future leaders.

"Design thinking" is a technique used to solve complex problems in today's fast-changing and highly competitive world, such as those faced by every company. A mindset of design is not product-focused- it is focused solution and action-oriented towards creating better experiences and value for the customer. It requires a new domestic culture and leadership in the industry.

Steve Jobs, at Apple, is perhaps the most known technology thought business leaders, moving the brand from personal computers to new markets, the iPad and iPhone included. Nevertheless, based on their latest studies, the function and criteria continue to evolve as outlined in a new book, "Innovation by Design," by Thomas Lockwood and Edgar Papke.

As an ambitious project thought manager or businessman, I follow their list of key criteria for you. Through my view, I'll paraphrase and summarize the top ten:

Make use of understanding to know the experiences of others. You will better understand the needs of people around you, including your customers and partners, by understanding experiences. It leads to loyalty, inspiration, and improved ability to persuade you from your point of view and pursue you despite the pain of transition and creativity.

Focus on creating a benefit for the customer. Holding the consumer-centered provides a shared understanding and cooperation for all with the intended outcome, as well as a move to higher rates of creativity. This emphasis also helps the group to better manage tension and dispute by reminding everyone of the common goal.

Listen with mutual respect and fearless exploration. Use design thinking as a tool not only improves your learning capacity, but also strengthens the ability to question and resolve conflicts. You should reframe challenging questions in a way that allows the team to recognize root cause challenges and implement more successful solutions.

Openly express ideas and what you think, see, and feel. It's not easy to give and receive feedback, particularly given that people will easily slip into defensive behavior patterns and feel sick at ease. Creative thinking leaders make challenging ideas secure, but keep the system and research-oriented rather than personal views.

Pursue knowledge by being curious and asking questions. Technology theorists become adventurers instead of being hierarchical. You learn by asking hard questions and getting the responses you get fearlessly. This makes it easier for all participants to find the right solution to dialog and mindset without undue emotion and conflict.

Demonstrate the ability to be vulnerable. Everybody understands that variability requires a higher degree of strength and courage, including the ability to accept your own mistakes and shortcomings. Leaders were exhibiting this skill in their positions as design experts are more relaxed and persuasive. For their fans, they become the standard.

Coach others, rather than competing with others. Coaching helps a person to increase self-awareness and adjust their role to better take advantage of their greatest strengths instead of highlighting and criticizing their weaknesses. As a leader, this fosters a constructive contribution rather than a protective debate on design ideas.

Rely on the knowledge and insight of others. Leaders in their company who promote innovation as a society can't afford to behave as the sole genius. Many team members have exclusive exposure and feedback to their clients as well as their own experiences. A ruler can only deal with the force multipliers by cooperation.

Use curious confrontation to manage disagreement and conflict. The curious rivalry is essentially the ability to explore and learn different concepts. This is a fundamental concept in design thinking, and the models for the rest of their group must be the experts in this area. We create healthy market differences and welcome them in driving creativity and progress that must be part of every successful business.

Align personal purpose with the organization's mission. More than marketing, mission-driven development is the mechanism that aligns the behavior, character, and environment of a company with its intent. For maximum credibility and impact, the best leaders can align their vision and choice power with the organization's mission.

Whether you're looking to continue your career as a business professional, or you're planning to take a leadership role in your own business, developing these key attributes will pay large dividends. None of these is right or require advanced degrees–anyone can study them.

They all play directly into another Megatrend that I see in business–moving from a single economic value bottom line to the triple economic, social, and environmental bottom line.

Visualization Tool

Visualization It's about using objects. It's not a painting, and it's mental imagery. It pushes us further than just using words or language. It's a way to unlock that aspect of our minds that helps us to think non-verbally and that administrators may not use regularly.

The rest of us will create our mental pictures as you describe an idea with language, normally told by our learning. The IT expert sees servers and software as you say, "We need a new growth plan," and the marketing guru sees an ad campaign. In drawing a picture of it instead, if you pose your proposal to us, you reduce the possibility of unparalleled mental models.

Journey mapping (or experience mapping) It is an ethnographic form of study that focuses on tracking the customer's "journey" as he or she engages with an entity when providing a service, with special attention to emotional highs and lows. Experience mapping is used to identify needs that customers are often unable to articulate.

A theoretical vision of what the experience of a certain consumer community looks like, even the part that doesn't include the business, is completed. Then hold pilot meetings with a select number of clients to ensure that you are recording the measures correctly. Furthermore, identify key points of reality and patterns from the interviews and describe a variety of aspects that you find are useful in understanding the gaps in the information you have obtained. The purpose is to create a collection of testing hypotheses.

Value chain analysis Examines how a company engages in creating, selling, and delivering new offerings to value chain partners. Value chain research offers ways to create better value for consumers along the chain and shows important clues about the strengths and goals of suppliers.

Documentation of the value chain is the source on the business side of consumer travel visualization. It begins by working backward by creating value for the ultimate end customer and then adding other primary suppliers ' skills and bargaining power.

Mind mapping Used to reflect whether and with each other concepts or other things are connected to a central idea. Mind maps are used for creating, visualizing, structuring, and classifying ideas to look for trends and observations that provide key criteria for development. We do this by showing the information and asking people to group them in ways that give rise to trends and patterns. Mind mapping must be a team sport to be successful.

Tap the visualization power to communicate and display as clearly and easily as possible the key components of what we have learned. Creating posters that capture key themes and trends in the data, then inviting a group of thoughtful people to tour the visual data and noticing any lessons they believe should inform new ideas, then clustering those lessons into themes. Look for clusters and insight connections. Ask the question, "Based on what we've heard, what characteristics would our model have if anything were possible?"

Rapid concept development It helps us to create potential new business opportunities ideas.

We take the design criteria, the consumer persona, and their pain points, and the value chain experiences that we have discovered through our work in the first phase, and use all of them to generate new ideas— many of them. We combine the suggestions into a convenient number of interesting topics in the second stage. Ultimately, in stage three, behind that set of ideas, we expand on the company model. We want to easily generate ideas and get them out to consumers to look at them as quickly as possible.

Assumption testing Focuses on defining the assumptions underlying the appeal of a new business concept and using available data to determine the probability that these hypotheses will be correct. Then, through thought experiments, these assumptions are tested, followed by field experiments.

Once you have decided which theories are most important to your new concept's future appeal, define evidence that helps you to check the main hypotheses conclusively. We identify the information we need here and then figure out how to get it.

Sort the data you need into one of three categories: what you know, what you don't know, and what you don't know, and what you don't know, but can't. The third class is paying to construct tests in thought. Identify what it would take to get the information rapidly, and plan your thought experiment, paying particular attention to the details that might prove you wrong.

Rapid prototyping Techniques enable us to provide potential partners and customers with abstract new ideas. These include storyboarding, user scenarios, traveling experiences, and illustrations of business concepts — all of which encourage the deep involvement of key stakeholders in providing feedback.

Prototyping aims to minimize "I" in ROI. A simple 2-D prototype might cost as little as a pen and some paper. Prototypes of the business concept take visual and narrative forms in general: images and stories. They can even include skills and role-playing. Use your prototype to play; don't defend it. Let it be validated by others— not the people who created it.

Customer creation Includes techniques that enable managers to engage their customers while generating and developing new business ideas of mutual interest. These are among the growth and development strategies that are most value-enhancing and risk-reducing.

We continue to be nervous about presenting incomplete, unpolished "things" to clients in our Six Sigma culture, which emphasizes consistency and shine. Get over it. Learning is about innovation, and customers have the most to teach us. The sooner we have something they can respond to in front of them, the sooner we get to a distinct value-added approach.

Engage one at a time, a dynamic and open network of consumers. Provide them with a visual stimulus, but at this stage, there is nothing fancy. Leaving missing parts of the design is a perfect way to attract the imagination and expertise of the consumers. Offer two or three choices and begin to discuss one to which they are drawn.

Learning launches Test the key underlying value-generating assumptions of a potential marketplace new-growth initiative. Unlike a full rollout of a new product, a learning launch is a learning experiment to gather market-driven data quickly and cheaply.

We call them launches rather than trials because both launcher and customers are supposed to feel real. Only then can reliable data be produced. They are an extension of the process of co-creation, but we are asking customers at this stage to put their money where their mouth is. People who say they're going to buy are just potential customers. The only true test of a customer idea's worth is their ability to part with cold hard cash.

Storytelling That's exactly how it sounds: weaving a story together instead of just making several points. It's a close visualization relative — another way to make new ideas feel real and compelling. In reality, visual storytelling is the most compelling story style. All fine, insightful, or design-oriented presentations tell a compelling tale.

Stories like images enable us to gain access to emotions and highlight experiences. They bring the complexity of meaning and allow us to "market" and solve a problem. They keep their audience awake with any luck.

Good stories are based on some basic principles: make sure your audience is identified. Creating a storyboard is critical; it helps us to pay close attention to motion and meaning. Set the scene to sell the question, make the cast of characters feel real, and work the plot; all good stories unfold with some suspense, and maybe some twists emerge— here's how to mix details and pictures to bring the points home. Unveil your resolution to the topic for the climax. Consider it spectacular. And don't hesitate to use metaphors, so analogies to make your story come alive!

Key Variables to Design a Large-Scale Organizational Transformation

In designing a large-scale organizational transformation, there are a lot of different elements. There are four areas to be explored to this organizational transformation for this exercise, and through the eyes of a consultant. These areas are human resources, structure of organization, leadership, and trust, and measures of performance. How these variables are implemented in the process of change could prove successful for an organization and help the organization's overall structure to grow. Also, lack of attention to detail can be a mistake and cause a process of change to fail.

Human Resources Policy

Human resources are the glue that holds the organization together, in the opinion of this writer.

Human resources contribute to policy enforcement and creation. Moreover, when something goes wrong or when a new benefit is introduced or when there is a change in the industry, they act as a front line. First, when an internal transition takes place, they serve as agents of change. Braun (2013) defines human resources as being more of a strategic partner than the paper pushers ' old paradigm. Therefore, human resources have accepted a higher calling in which they assist with all corporate tasks, help formulate strategies, create long-term goals, and execute plans to help build a competitive advantage in the marketplace. The goal is to understand change as a consultant and working with human resources. According to Appelbaum, Berke, Taylor, and Vazquez (2008), change is viewed as a dynamic process and can be assessed in terms of a change's scale and which method will be involved. Human resources and the organization's leaders must take into account how this transformation on a large scale will affect the policies in place. Will the compensation process, for instance, be modified from a generic appraisal to a more complex performance management system?

The company is cited by its author is undergoing a major transition. The program of bonus and payment package was a strong tool, and any pay increases were suspended for the last three fiscal years. However, most services and incentives have also been cut to reduce the organization's expenses. These policy changes were a necessary evil to help restore the organization's structure. This change in organizational policy has caused a lot of employee engagement issues, and it has been difficult to retain top talent, but at the moment the storm has been weathered, and the policies and benefits of organizations are returning to normal as new initiatives are taking place.

Organizational Structure

Understanding how an organization is structured is a key goal for a consultancy that supports organizational transformation. To name a few, the consultant must understand whether the organization is transformative, top-down, transactional, growth, mature, global, and local. Appelbaum et al. (2008) describe transformation as a form of corporate change and can be described as a process of development and is a form of revolutionary change that can be described as a complete re-engineering of the corporate structure. As a consultant, understanding the organization's goals is important, but also providing solutions, and the need for transformational leadership comes with transformative change. Transformation leadership leads to the status quo and the success of the company by motivating its workers to do more and lead by example. Damanpour and Wischnevsky (2006) examined organizational transformation and claimed that organizational transformation is a transition of structure and plan between organizational states. To help in the re-engineering of the organizational structure, management will be empowered to redefine policy, update the mission statement, and eventually rebrand it with a new logo that separates the organization from the existing one and opens the door to the new era of growth and prospects.

Within the company discussed in this exercise, one of their top goals is transformational leadership and a community they try to establish. Unfortunately, they lack the follow-up and the learning of the organization to continue the process of changing the culture internally. Due to high turnover in leadership positions, it is very difficult to develop a philosophy that will be rooted in the history of the company.

Leadership Communication

Unless all the necessary stakeholders are on board and understand the new mission, organizational transformation cannot begin. The company would run into resistance to change without adequate and consistent contact with leaders/managers and their direct reports. The aim of interaction with leadership is to get members closer to the company and to give them a sense of belonging and meaning. Brauns (2013) provides examples of how corporate transition from performance management would look like to encourage keeping workers informed, and retaining employees involved during the shift should be a priority. The incentive system in place, for instance, needs to express the organization's ideals and should send the right message from an institutional viewpoint. If employees do not understand the value of the rewards or benefits, there will be resistance to change. However, performance management has to be discussed and according to Brauns (2013) consists of the three C's, continuity, communication, and control. If leadership can communicate and gain their organization's and followers ' trust, this will make transformation more achievable on a large scale.

Without confidence, employee resistance will hamper any effect of change.

With this field of transition, the company that is the guide for the project has not done a very good job. During the recovery process, there seems to be little concern for job descriptions or compensation. Although there are numerous attempts to bring about positive reform and provide guidance into progressive leadership, they do not have the follow-up to succeed to make the necessary difference. At times, messages with management are confused and unclear, which can exacerbate workplace dissatisfaction. Regular contact and often feedback on the success of the change process would be suggested. Stability from within is short, with the emergence of several key leaders over the past six months.

Performance Measure

Quality measures are needed to ensure that the company meets its targets on a large scale but also that the internal expectations of its workers are achieved. Chen, Yang, and Jiun (2006) investigated the Balances Scorecard or BSC performance management system. BSC allows businesses to change their overall strategy and provide active leadership and management. This is achieved by addressing four perspectives. These are economical, consumer, social, and learning fields of insight.

In-house, the customer and learning were addressed as major components of organizational transformation throughout this exercise. Although the financial viewpoint is not discussed by name, it is inferred to have a stable enterprise and to reach that equilibrium through a significant transition.

We do have their performance management program in the business cited, although it seems to be very focused on individual metrics and expectations in which this author sounds very unspecific and abstract. Furthermore, without a system of rewards in place, a system of performance management seems silent. This author advises that a minor reward be added to the output metric otherwise the outcome is black or white; either you meet the requirements and keep your job, or you are fired. Leadership is tasked with keeping the organization's dedication strong and providing excellent interaction to retain a productive workforce during the large-scale transition shift. Without this leadership guidance and the employees ' input, which is considered a critical factor, according to Appelbaum et al. (2008), it will be difficult to achieve large-scale transformation change.

Conclusion

To remain competitive in the industry, companies need to adapt. Whether they learn and use the learned knowledge would surely give them a competitive advantage over their rivals. The organization needs to pay attention to human resource policies, communication of leadership, organizational structure, and performance management systems to complete a large-scale change. In shaping a successful transformation, all these areas play important roles.

Conclusion

A comprehensive approach to solving business problems is the design process with its elements of open idea generation, multidisciplinary collaboration, prototyping, execution and continuous refinement. But most businesses don't use it, and worse still, most business schools don't teach it.

Design thinking, combined with group collaboration, is essentially a user-centric approach, project-based workflow, inductive, deductive and abductive reasoning. The goal of the design process, instead of focusing solely on analytics and rigorous quantitative analysis, is to generate ideas that keep the customer in mind. It involves an almost anthropological insight into how the user perceives, interacts and uses the product or service and how these actions and reactions can best be optimized.

To catalyze creativity, Design Thinking connects policy and implementation. This article identifies one aspect of Design Thinking called Making Thinking Visible-a user-friendly framework for overcoming issues that separate people who are tasked with working in teams so that they can think, decide and execute together. It is a strategy for immediate assessment and feedback to be given and received.

Making Thought Visible is focused on constructive dialogue between participants (information, topics, documentation creators, system witnesses, and those who have not engaged in any of these–colleagues, administrators, clients, and consumers) at various points of contact to understand the array of common visual media.

Although analysis is part of any report of investigation, it makes it clear. His deliberate visibility calls for scrutiny, comparison, and lively discussion. Building participant's co-constructors of the knowledge base bridge disciplines and diversity of view more organically. A director who knew her staff very well later told me that she was "surprised to see the variety of solutions" that they had come up with. As writer Peter Cairo says, involving the "brain, heart and guts" instinctively creates buy-in and is a competitive advantage today.

Shared visual media dissolve tension so that people move more quickly through the normal (stuck) appraisal quagmires. "This promotes active attention," as a respondent said. People get to know each other in an unforced manner so that there is more trust for those outsides of our training and in the normal way of thinking and doing.

Making Thinking Visible has an in-house aspect that is unedited and an edited, public aspect. It deliberately reveals the back story of an inquiry in a safe context- the gaff, errors, "let's not go there again" moments- moving beyond cosmetics to learning meaningful experiences. It sounds simple, yet there are few mechanisms for making mistakes as a generative act. The aim is to fail easily, always, and with others who do the same for an inquiry subject. The surface of the team is jells and best practices. We get acclimatized to start quickly without making a fuss again. Skateboarders are excellent here.

Printed in Great Britain
by Amazon

36181699R00108